From Log Cabin to the Pulpit; or, Fifteen Years in Slavery

Rev. W. H. Robinson

FROM LOG CABIN TO THE PULPIT,

OR,

FIFTEEN YEARS IN SLAVERY

THIRD EDITION

PUBLISHED BY THE AUTHOR,

REV. W. H. ROBINSON,

REMINISCENCES OF MY EARLY LIFE WHILE IN SLAVERY.

DEDICATED TO MY DAUGHTER, MARGUERITE.

1913.

CONTENTS

OLD GLORY!

The old tattered flag, that passed through the siege of the "Civil War" which freed the colored race from slavery and saved the Union from disruption. The old flag was fought under by the colored as well as the white boys, and was preserved as the Nation's emblem of freedom. "Long may it wave o'er the land of the free and the home of the brave."

PRESENTATION.

I present this work to the public on it's merits; there is no fiction about it, every incident is taken from reality. The author has either pasted through or been an eye witness to every trying ordeal and incident, with a very few exceptions, and he has authentic history to sustain him in these. Every line is dictated by the author, W. H Robinson, and written by his secretary, Miss Florence Mitchell, of Louisville, Kentucky.

"FROM Log Cabin To The PULPIT" OR "FIFTEEN YEARS IN SLAVERY"

ENDORSEMENTS.

Having read the within pages I can conscientiously recommend the book as being of intense interest from first to last; full of interesting narrative, valuable historical information, good suggestions and wholesome inspiration. It is more than worth the price asked for it.

J. M. GASS,
Editor "News," Albia, Iowa.

April 14, 1913.

To Whom It May Concern:

It gives me pleasure to be permitted to state that the Rev. W. H. Robinson is personally known to me as a man whom God is most wonderfully using in the extension of His Kingdom. He is most favorably known in the state and enjoys the highest esteem of the churches. His evangelistic labors have been signally successful, churches being quickened, church members reclaimed and large numbers truly converted. His book I consider, of great value, presenting as it does, a vivid and truthful story of the remarkable manner in which God by his grace, can use one who is consecrated to the service of the Master

Yours very truly,
GEO. R. STAIR,
Pastor First Baptist Church, Eau Claire, Wisconsin.

REV. W. H. ROBINSON, AUTHOR.

AUTHOR'S PREFACE.

My friends, it is not the purpose of the writer to place before the public something to bias the minds of the people or instill a spirit of hatred. My book reveals in every chapter either the pathetic moan of slaves in almost utter despair, yet panting, groaning, bitterly wailing and still hoping for freedom, or of slaves with their hearts, lifted to God, praying for deliverance from the cruel bonds, the auction block, and years of unrequited grinding toil for those who had no right to their labor.

Realizing, as I do, the injunction of the Lord Jesus, when he said, in Matthew VII, 12: "Therefore, all things whatsoever ye would that men should do to you, do ye so to them, for this is the law and the prophets" my deliberations have been many and constant that God would take out of my heart all the spirit of retaliation or revenge. This is why my book has not been before the public years ago. I wanted to be assured of the fact that I could give to the world at least some thoughts that would not only be a remembrance, but would prove beneficial to all in whose hands this book may chance to fall. I would not have this all important fact pass from the mind and memory of men, that they should not give their consent, nor cast their ballot for the enslavement of any human being.

To some of the noble men of this country, yea to many whose blood has stained the earth at Fairfax Courthouse, Virginia, Roanoke Island, North Carolina, Fort Donelson, Pea Ridge Arkansas, Shiloh or Pittsburg Landing, Tennessee, Williamsburg, Virginia, and many other places too numerous to mention, it is but as yesterday since the noble men, who are sleeping in unknown graves, left their homes and loved ones to lay their lives on the sacrificial altar of their country, to perpetuate this government and help to shake the shackles of bondage from a race hewn from a slab of ebony. It is but yesterday, in our memories, since mothers gave their only sons, wives their husbands, sisters their brothers, sweethearts their intended, to take part in shaking the manacles from this unfortunate race. It is but yesterday since the sad message came that many of those loved ones had fallen in the forefront of the battle, saturated in their own blood, fighting for human liberty.

Gratitude will not pay for the loss of those dear ones, nor for those who returned limbless, and with shattered health, but it is the greatest gift in human reach. May God ever bless. and he will bless, the Caucasian race for the Moses, in the person of an Abraham Lincoln, who led us across the Red Sea of slavery into the promised land of liberty, where today we can worship God under our own vine and fig tree, and no one dare molest us or make us afraid.

Having given you this short preface I will at once proceed to give you a history of my life as a slave, and of slavery from a historical standpoint; also eleven months of my life in England, where I received my first alphabetical training.

The Late Mrs. W H. Robinson

CHAPTER I.

I was born in Wilmington, a town in North Carolina, March 11, 1848. Wilmington is situated near the mouth of the Cape Fear river, on the Atlantic coast. It has a good harbor on the tidal waters of Cape Fear river. The chief exports are cotton and tobacco from the uplands, and lumber, rosin and turpentine from the yellow pine forests of the coastal plains. The swampy coastal lowlands produce great quantities of rice.

In reading Stanley and Livingston on Africa we notice that the negro race is divided into different tribes. Among them is the Madagascar tribe, who are noted for their mechanical skill. To this tribe my parents both belonged.

My parents, Peter and Rosy, belonged to a very wealthy ship and slave holder, who owned two farms and over five hundred slaves.

My father was an engineer and towed vessels in and out of Wilmington harbor into the Atlantic ocean. He pursued this occupation for over fifteen years and received many tips by being courteous and always on the alert for ships heaving in sight. While the master received pay for the towage, my father by constant contact with white men, received money in many other ways. "As association breeds assimilation" so my father learned the art of making and saving money until he had accumulated about eleven hundred dollars.

My mother was a cook at the great house, but hired her time from her mistress, for which she paid three dollars per month.

It becomes necessary to explain how slaves would get money to pay for their time There were shipped from Wilmington a great many ground-peas or peanuts, as we now call them. They were brought from the country in bulk and so had to he sacked and sewed up. The slaves were hired for this work, for which they received one cent and a half per sack. This is one of the great mediums through which they

1

made money. Another was, a great many hogsheads of molasses were brought from New Orleans and unloaded on the docks, and the hot sun would cause them to ferment and run out through the chimes. The negro women would catch this molasses by running their hands over the hogshead and wiping the molasses from their hands into a pail. I am often made to wonder now when I see people gagging at the idea of eating bread made up by black hands, when in those days the poor whites were truly glad to buy the molasses caught in the hands of our mothers, and like Elijah, who was fed by the ravens, they ate it and asked no questions.

Father enjoyed the friendship of two very distinguished Quakers, Mr. Fuller and Mr. Elliott, who owned oyster sloops, and stood at the head of what is known in our country as the underground railroad, or an organization filled with love of freedom for suffering humanity, that had for its end the liberation of slaves and that only. Hundreds of men belonging to this organization sacrificed their lives in carrying out this noble purpose.

Father was with Messrs Fuller and Elliott every day towing them in and out from the oyster bay. This gave them an opportunity to lay and devise plans for getting many into Canada (the only safe refuge for the negro this side the Atlantic.) and my father was an important factor in this line.

The system of deliverance by the underground railroad was to divide the country off into sections, and at every fifteen or twenty miles would be a station or depot. One man would haul the slaves at night to the end of his station and get back home before daylight, undiscovered, then they would be conveyed the next night in wagons from that station to the next, and so on until they reached Canada.

Often the wagons had double linings, with corn or wheat visible, while the cavity was filled with women and children.

Father having a foretaste of liberty to some extent, and growing weary of the life of a slave, with the assistance of his Quaker friends plans were laid for him to purchase his own freedom and go to Canada. Then his family would be sent to him by the underground railroad. If any one connected with the underground railroad was caught the penalty was a heavy fine and expulsion from the state.

Allow me to state here that in 1875, while on the train going to Wilmington, North Carolina, in search of a sister and brother, I met a white man having the appearance of a lawyer. He talked very freely with me and I soon learned that he was from Boston, Massachusetts, and that he was a merchant instead of a lawyer. His continued conversation with me attracted the attention of nearly all the passengers in the car, and they were not careful or considerate in their criticism, for they were heard to say several times, "he is a Northern negro lover," or, "one of Lincoln's hirelings," and such like expressions We were truly glad when we reached Wilmington and could get away from the scrutinizing eyes and listening ears of the passengers in the car. He asked me if Wilmington was my home. I told him it was, but that I did not love a grain of sand of that soil. He assured me that this was the case with him, for said he, "my father lost his life here trying to help a colored man to liberty." I asked him who his father was. He said, "Sam Fuller." When he learned that I had known his father from my childhood days it seemed to draw him closer to me, and we were both dumbfounded for a moment when it was made known that his father had lost his life because he had tried to help my father secure his freedom. We both broke down and wept for a few moments, but I recognized the danger we were in, even in 1875, in a southern state. So we parted with the understanding that we keep in touch with each other until we got to Indianapolis, Indiana. As there was danger of both being murdered we passed each other almost as strangers on the streets of Wilmington for over a week, and finally we both left on the same train. We spent a week together in the city of Indianapolis, Indiana. From the way he spent money on me it seemed that he thought he owed me some gratitude instead of my owing it to him.

He now told me the story of the death of his father and how it came about. My master became suspicious, or mistrusted from surrounding circumstances, that Mr. Fuller was the deviser of father's attempt to buy his freedom. A few nights after father was sold from Wilmington a posse of men notified Mr. Fuller to leave the state at once, and they left a crossbone and skull on a stick in front of his door. He left his wife and four children, Samuel, Jr., the man I met on the train being the oldest, with the understanding that he would send for them in a few days. He has never been heard from since. The supposition is that he was murdered. The family remained there until the rebellion, when they left for Indiana, afterward going from there to Massachusetts.

The young man's business in Wilmington was to look after the little homestead, which was about forty acres of land. I was not successful in finding my sister and brother, but felt amply paid by meeting an old friend to the negro race and one who helped my father in many different ways.

CHAPTER II.

The plans to free father were put into execution in 1858 My father went to his master to ascertain what he would take for him. The first question master asked him was, what white man had put him up to this? His suspicion at once fell on these two Quakers. Father finally succeeded in convincing him that no white man was implicated. Then his next question was, "how much money have you?" Father told him $450, so he agreed to take $1,150 for him. This was an exorbitant price and he didn't think father would ever be able to pay it. He could have paid him the amount down, but in counsel the Quakers had thought it would not be the best thing to do for fear it would confuse the whole plan and jeopardize their lives.

He was to pay for himself on the installment plan, paying $450 down, with the understanding that he continue six months on the tug to teach another man to run it, then he could work wherever he pleased. Every year he was to pay as much as he could, which he did, together with the interest.

At this time the subject of slavery was being greatly agitated in the north, and slaves were depreciating in value. In 1859 my father went to California with a surveying company, staying one year. He returned during the holidays, paying $350 more on himself, making a total of $800 paid on his debt. He went back to California after the holidays and was gone about three months, when the news came to us that he was returning in chains. We knew exactly what that meant; to rob him of what he had paid and sell him away from us, and we were not mistaken, for this was the exact purpose.

You may wonder how we received the news, knowing we had no access to the telegraph or postoffice. Now, to explain this. To get news from one farm to another one slave would tell the other, and so on, until by this means and that of the underground railroad, it would reach it's destination. So father sent us the news in this way, clear from California to North Carolina.

For two months we went every day when the boat came, to see if father was on it. At last the sad hour came when the boat arrived, bringing father bound in chains. We saw him pulling his whiskers (a mark of deep sorrow with him.) When they took him off the boat we found he had worn handcuffs fourteen days and his ankles, from the manacles, were as raw as a piece of beef.

That night they took him to the jail, or negro pen, and there we left them trying to unlock the handcuffs, for the flesh had swollen so it made it almost impossible to unlock them. The negro trader ordered mother and five of us children to go home, assuring us that we would see father in the morning.

That night I saw mother in every attitude of prayer a human being could assume. Sometimes she would be prostrate upon her face on the floor; sometimes on her knees and again in a sitting posture, imploring God to use his power in some way to keep father from being sold from us.

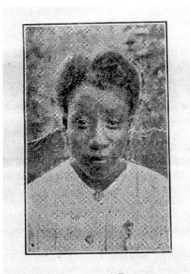

Miss MARGUERITE ROBINSON.

Then about twelve o'clock that night mother said we would go to the great house, and so we went, notwithstanding the rigidness of the law; for there was a standing law, that any negro caught out after nine o'clock at night should be struck thirty-nine lashes. But now, as the war was dawning, they were more rigid than ever, and raised it to forty-nine lashes.

CHAPTER III.

There were four classes of men who made their living on the blood of the negro The first class is the master proper. He feels himself too honorable to drive the slave from two or three o'clock in the morning until nine or ten at night, therefore he sees the necessity of the second class, so he hires a poor white man as overseer, to do this dirty work.

The overseer had the authority, if the slave - man, woman or child - failed to do his task, to tie him up and whip him, but not to exceed one hundred and fifty lashes. If the crime demanded more than that he must get special authority from the master. The punishment, as will he shown further on, was very high for trivial offenses.

Sometimes the task was too heavy for the negro and he could not complete it, and would rise up in his manhood and would not be whipped. Then his only alternative was to run away, and this usually was the first thought in his mind. The third man raised blood hounds and trained them to hunt nothing but negroes. He made his living by catching runaway negroes, receiving the paltry sum of three dollars per head. The fourth man is the negro trader, who made a perpetual business of buying and selling negroes, as men do cattle in this country. He would buy up eight, ten or twenty, as the case might be, and locate them at some central point until he had from three to five hundred. Then he would have a long chain and handcuff them on either side of the chain and march them to Richmond, Virginia, which was the central slave market of the south, owned and conducted by the Lees and known as Lee's negro trader's pen, and when there they would auction them off to the highest bidder.

The prosperity of the poor whites, with but few exceptions, depended upon the amount of brutality that be showed towards the negro. His word was not valued as highly as that of the negro if it was not in favor with that of his employer. He lived in no better homes, and many of them not as good as the negro quarters. I need not say that they had but little or no aspirations, save that of raising blood hounds to catch the slaves with when they ran away. They were usually very illiterate, many of them had no education at all; they had no association only among themselves and the negroes. Their wives were glad to do the drudgery for that class of whites who would not own slaves. There were no free school systems, and they had not aspirations enough to pay for schooling their children. When they went before their employer they put their hats under their arms, as any negro would do, and usually were as afraid of him as the negro was of the overseer. They dressed as hideously as they possibly could in order to strike terror to the hearts of the negroes; they wore broad brimmed slouch hats, their pants down in their boots and a long blacksnake whip across their shoulders; they trained their voices to be as harsh as possible. Their very appearance would cause one to shiver. Their living was not as good as that of the average negro, for the slaves were industrious and would work by the light of the moon to earn a few pennies, while the overseer was lazy and seemed to be satisfied with most any kind of fare.

Every week he drew a certain amount of fat meat, corn meal, and a little flour from his master's smoke houses just the same as the slaves did. He often hired the slaves to steal hogs or chickens for him and if caught the slaves would have to take it all upon themselves in order to keep the good will of the overseer. They used the same dialect as the negro in every respect. While the negro looked for a day of deliverance the overseer looked for nothing. He was at the height of his ambition while driving the negro.

CHAPTER IV.

Let us go back to the "great house" where we left my mother. She awoke Master Tom and thought she would reach him through his religious views, so she said: "Master Tom, have you forgotten your religion? Have you the heart to sell my husband from me and my children after he has served you all these days and made you a fortune?" He said, "No, Rosy, I've nothing to do with that. Your husband is in the hands of the state of California, but I'll see that he is not taken out of this state."

Of course he knew that mother was ignorant as to the laws of the state, that he would have had to have been tried in the state where the offense was committed had there been any offense, but this was only a pretext he used to rob her of her husband, and her children of their father; the father of his money and liberty.

Mother asked why he was brought back as a slave when he was buying himself and had already paid eight hundred dollars. He told her that father had become intimate with a white lady. (She could not have been a lady and be intimate with a negro, and that negro a slave.) After assuring mother that father would not again be taken out of the state, Master Tom wrote us a pass and we went back home.

About three a. m. mother concluded we had better go to the jail, so we went, and saw father standing at the window. I called him once, but he waved his hand to us, as if to tell us some one was down stairs, and motioned for us to go back home.

Mother cooked a good breakfast for him, and between eight and nine o'clock we went back to the negro trader's pen, but before we got there we heard singing of two clases. Some religious songs, such as "God has delivered Daniel," and other melodies, while others were singing the songs of the world, all seemingly rejoicing in their own way. Some were rejoicing because they were sold, hoping to fall into the hands of better masters, while others were rejoicing because of the hope of meeting their mother, father or child.

We knew exactly what that meant; we knew that the number was complete and about to start for Richmond, and we were not mistaken, for there were three hundred men, women and children ready to start within thirty minutes from the time we got there. We hastily scanned the line over for father, but he was not in that gang. But there was a vehicle built something like our omnibuses, which convey passengers from the depot, only it was built of heavy oak boards, with staples driven in them. They would handcuff men that were valuable and men that would not be whipped. I climbed upon the wheel of this vehicle and saw father sitting with his face buried in his hands. As I spoke he came to the iron grating or window, and asked where mother was. I told him she was there, then he said to me, "William, never pull off your shirt to be whipped. I want you to die in defense of your mother; for once I lay in the woods eleven months for trying to prevent your mother from being whipped." He shook my hands and kissed me good bye through the iron bars. Then three sisters and two brothers climbed upon the wheel and bade him good bye. Now the most trying scene of all is at hand. Mother climbed upon the wheel and father said, "Rosy, I'm bound for Richmond, Virginia, and from there to some Southern market, I don't know where. We may never meet again this side of the shores of time, hut Rosy, keep the faith in God, and meet me in heaven. I want this one assurance from you before we part: I want to know if you believe the charge brought against me, for which they are robbing me of my liberty?" My mother assured him she did not believe it.

The trader came up, ordered mother down from the wheel, and the vehicle to start. Father kissed her good bye, with a mutual agreement that they would never marry any one else, even though they never met again. Forty years passed into eternity from that sad hour until mother's death, in 1898, and father and mother never met again until they met on the other shore.

This was the beginning, of sorrow in our home. It was not over three weeks from the time that father was sold away until mother and three children were taken to the great house, and the other children scattered around on the different farms. I was taken into the house to wait on table.

About a month after I entered upon my new occupation my master told me one day, while sitting on the porch, to light his pipe. He smoked a pipe with a long reed stem and would rest the bowl of it on a shelf. After I lit the pipe he ordered me to bring him a glass of water. I went for it, but on returning I found he had turned a sallow complexion. I spoke to him but he did not answer. I called old mistress, (this is the way we distinguished her from the children, as we called all, from the least to the biggest, mistress and master.) She came and spoke to him, but there was no reply. He had died sitting there in his chair.

It was the custom among the slave holders to have the older slaves come and view the remains of their masters or mistresses while they lay in state, and if the master was an man of any humanity, or what we termed a good master, they would actually shed tears over his body. So as usual, they called the slaves in, but old mistress did not know that Master Tom had incurred the ill-will of every slave on the place by selling father.

Father was almost a prophet among my people, because he secured all the news through his Quaker friends, and other white men that were friendly to him, with whom he came in contact. Then he would tell it to our people. Of course the slaves held him in high esteem, and when Master Tom sold him they never again had any good feeling for him. They came as usual, but just outside the door they wet their fingers with saliva and made "crocodile tears" and passed on pretending to be crying, and saying, "Poor Massa Tom is gone." Of course they didn't say where he had gone.

This may appear very deceptive, but had we not made some demonstration of grief our very lives would have been in danger.

CHAPTER V.

About three weeks later they began to look up the will, for boys then were like a good many are today, just waiting for the old man to die, so they could run through with what he had accumulated. We have many young men of that class today. They are not worthy to bear their father's name. It was found in the will that mother and three of the children had fallen to Scott Cowens - the meanest of all the Cowens family. He was a drunkard and a gambler, for he had taken three different women's sons, between the ages of twelve and fourteen years, and gambled them off and came back home without them, leaving the parents in anguish, We went to his home, mother as cook, the rest as servants in general.

We had been there but a few months when he called my mother one day and asked her why she said "that God had sent swift judgment upon his father." Of course mother denied it, but in her grief she had thoughtlessly said it, and somehow it had reached his ears. He threatened mother very strongly, but didn't strike her.

He left home one evening, telling me to be ready to accompany him when he returned. He did not come back until the next morning. I saw at once that he had been drinking heavily. He sat down to the breakfast table and ordered me to bring him a glass of cool water right from the spring. I put the glass of water in front of him. He immediately picked it up and threw the water in my face, saying "I will show you how to bring me dirty water to drink."

One morning a few days later, he found fault with the biscuits and asked me what was the matter with them. I told him I didn't know. He then jumped up from the table and called mother. We, from the least to the largest, were taught when called by our mistress, or master to answer and go toward that voice. So mother was coming to him and he met her on the porch, between the kitchen and the dining room. He asked mother why she was crying - I had told her about his throwing the water in my face - and before she could answer him he knocked her from the porch to the ground. This was

13

more than I could endure. An ax handle was on the opposite side from which mother fell. He stood over her, cursing and kicking her, and I knocked him down with the ax handle.

I knew my only hope of escape was to run away, so I started at once. I had often heard ex-runaway slaves, men and women, tell the adventures of when they were in the woods and about their hiding places or rendezvous. I had heard it told so often at my father's fireside that I knew almost directly where they were, for I had passed close by them many times, so I started to look for them. I went to the three mile farm, arriving there about the time they were going to dinner. I went to an old mother - we were taught to call each old woman mother, and they called us son or daughter. It seemed there was a natural bond of sympathy existing in the heart of every woman for the children of others. I told her what I had done. She gave me a chunk of fat meat and half of a corn dodger and directed me the way to a hiding place. Then with her hand upon my head she prayed one of those fervent prayers for God to hasten the day when the cruel chains of slavery would fall, and women's children would not be forced to leave home and take refuge among the beasts of the forest for trying to protect their mothers.

Quite late that night I got opposite the hiding place. It was a low swampy place back of a thick cane brake. It was so dark and the cane so thick when I got to the place where I had been directed to turn in I was afraid to venture. But as I stood there I imagined I could hear the baying of blood hounds, and so strong was the imagination that it drove me in. I had several things to fear, for that country was infested with bears. More than once I had seen a bear come out of a corn field with his arms full of corn, go up to the fence and throw it over, get over, pick it up like a man, and walk off. Then we had reptiles, such as water moccasins and rattle snakes. Sometimes I could walk upright, sometimes I was compelled to crawl through the cane. About three o'clock the next morning I came out of the cane brake on the banks of a large pond of almost stagnant water. I could see the rocky mound or cave that I had heard so much talk of.

There was no boat around and I was afraid to go into the water, but the same impulse that drove me into the cane brake caused me to go into the water. With a long reed for a staff I waded into the water until I heard the voice of a man, in the real coarse negro dialect, "who is dat?" My hair was not extremely long, yet it seemed so to me, as I imagined I felt my hat going up, and I answered "dis is me." (Of course he knew who "me" was.) He then began to question me as to my name and my parents' name. It was necessary for him to be very cautious whom he admitted, because white men often disguised themselves and played the role of a runaway, and in this way many runaways had been captured. I finally succeeded in convincing him that I was not a spy but an actual runaway. Then he allowed me to advance, and as I sat on the top of the rocky mound with him he prayed long and earnestly for the time to come when God would raise up a deliverer to lead us in some way out of bondage. And while he was thus praying I heard this peculiar sound, "gaw goo." The old man saw I was in a terrible dilemma, and he said, "son, you need not be uneasy, that is only some men below snoring." In a few minutes I looked across the field and saw two men coming with poles on their backs, and I got excited again, and called his attention to the fact. He assured me that they were men who had been off seeking food. They were stealing.

Our people in those days were naturally good hunters, but never shot anything larger than a coon nor smaller than a chicken, always good on the wing with the latter. They threw their game down. It consisted of some fat hens and meat they had returned to their homes and secured.

There was always an understanding between the slaves, that if one ran away they would put something to eat at a certain place; also a mowing scythe, with the crooked handle replaced with a straight stick with which to fight the bloodhounds.

The cook came out, made a hot fire of hickory bark, thoroughly wet the chickens and wrapped them in cabbage leaves and put them in the bed of ashes; then he proceeded to make his bread by mixing the corn meal in an old wooden tray and forming it into dodgers, rolling them in cabbage leaves and baking in the ashes. These are known as ash cakes, the most nutritious bread ever eaten. Of course the chickens retained all their nutriment because the intestines had not been taken out of them. But now he returned to them and catching them by both feet he stripped the skin and feathers off, then took the intestines out and put red pepper and salt in them and then returned them to the oven to brown. Parched some corn meal for coffee. Breakfast being ready, the guests came from the sleeping place, fifteen in number, the two huntsmen made seventeen, the old man and myself making nineteen in all, all runaways.

Among them was a man named Frank Anderson. His father, James Anderson, a white man of Wilmington, was his master. Yet he was a runaway slave, with a standing reward of one hundred dollars for his head.

He had been a fugitive eleven months, and had stripes on his back like the ridges of a wash board, put there by his father's overseer and by the command of that father, simply because he had so much of his father's blood in him that he would not allow them to lacerate his back only when they overpowered him.

MISS FLORENCE MITCHELL, SECRETARY,
Louisville, Ky.

CHAPTER VI.

Uncle Amos, as the watchman was called, was a prophet among us. He would watch every night, and took me as his companion, as I was the only boy. So I slept in the day and watched with him at night. He was a great astrologer, although he could not read a word; but strange to say, he would go out and lie flat on his back and watch the moon and stars, go through some peculiar movement with his hands, then the next morning he could tell almost anything you wanted to know. Many times it came just as he prophesied.

One morning, after I had been to the hiding place about three weeks, the runaways inquired, as was the custom. "if everything was all right, or what would happen." If he answered them in the affirmative, they were perfectly satisfied with his decision. But on this memorable morning he told them that we would have to get away at once, for if we did not we would be attacked within three days by negro hunters, for said he, "God has shown me the hounds and the men, and that some one will lose his life if the attack is made here."

So they decided to go to another rendezvous fourteen miles away. Uncle Amos advised each one to get his weapon in shape, and get provisions enough that night to last a few days, or until they learned something about the country surrounding the other hiding place.

When men ran away, if in the day, they returned at night and secured a mowing scythe and took the crooked handle off and put a straight handle on it. Then they made a scabbard of bark, and would swing their saber to their side. This was to fight blood hounds with, and if the negro hunters got too close, many times they were hew ndown.

On that night three different parties were out foraging, and returned with considerable provisions. But the next morning, while we were eating breakfast, negro hunters suddenly appeared with shot guns and drawn revolvers, and demanded every one of us to wade over to them. They had negro men to hold the hounds and cut the cane so they could pass through. These men had worked noiselessly all night, cutting the way through the cane.

I told Uncle Amos several times that I thought I heard something, but he seemed to think it more fear in me than reality, and he failed to give the proper attention.

We all jumped to our feet, with instructions from the old man to march over in a body, and each choose his man and dog to cut down when they reached the other shore, but the hunters were on the alert and demanded all to stand in a row, then march over one at a time. One of the hunters said to Frank Anderson, "if you run I'll blow your brains out." We formed a line and in a moment Frank Anderson bounded off like a deer. We heard the crack of a gun, saw Frank throw up both his hands and fall, and in a minute he lay cold in death. Murdered because he wouldn't consent to be tied up and whipped when he was late returning home from a Saturday night dance.

One by one we all marched over and were handcuffed to each other and marched off to the road, and the colored men who were with the hunters carried Frank over and put him in the mule cart which they had with them, and he could he tracked for thirteen miles by the blood which dropped through the cracks in the cart. His father rode over the sand stained by the blood of his son, whom he had commanded to be murdered.

This is but a small portion of the horrors through which my people passed. No tongue has ever been able to utter, nor has the pen been forged that can pen the horrors through which my people have passed. But they kept a constant knocking by faith at mercy's door, until God moved in his mighty power and touched the heart of Lincoln, who was a type of a second Moses, through whom he delivered us. They surrendered us to the jailor or keeper of the negro pen. There was no jail after all, only negro pens for slaves. If a poor white man transgressed the law, they simply took what he had and gave him time to get out of the country. The Lords, who were our masters, hoodwinked the law. If the negro transgressed, he paid the penalty with a lacerated back, from fifty to three hundred lashes. So you see there was no need for jails, only negro pens where slaves were bought and sold as goods and chattels.

These men received for capturing us the paltry sum of three dollars per head as the reward for the capture of runaway negroes, and the additional two hundred offered for the head of Frank Anderson, which had been a standing reward from his master, as be couldn't be captured in the first six months after he ran away. This was equivalent to his father's saying that it was better his own son should die than have all the other negroes spoiled. Nearly all of us were struck thirty-nine lashes according to the law, then returned to our several masters.

For some cause I was among the few exempted from the thirty-nine lashes. My master paid the stipulated amount of three dollars and ordered me home. I walked off in front of him under a storm of oaths and threats, and expecting him to kick me or knock me down at every step. But I was agreeably disappointed.

REV. W. H. ROBINSON
AND DAUGHTER, MARGUERITE.

CHAPTER VII.

When I arrived home I found that my mother, one brother and one sister that were with her when I left, had been sold to negro traders, and three brothers who fell to Hezekiah Cowens were also sold away, and no one could tell me anything about their whereabouts. Of course my master wouldn't tell me. This was the hour of great sorrow and distress with me. My master gave me the task of piling up stove wood, and for three weeks nearly every stick of wood I picked up was wet with tears of grief and sorrow, weeping for that mother who was the best friend on earth to me, and for my brothers and sisters, and expecting every day to be whipped. And this suspense was one of the most severe punishments or whippings I could have undergone.

There was another old woman whom I called mother, doing the cooking. One day at the expiration of the third week, master sent me to the store to get some goods, and in the packages there was a cow-hide in its crude state, but I didn't see it wrapped up. After unwrapping the cow-hide my master asked me how I liked the looks of it. I told him that I didn't like it at all. We were in his bed room. He stood between me and the door. His wife came in with his decanter of whiskey, glass and water and he locked the door, then demanded me to pull off my shirt. I had not forgotten the promise I made my father, so I fully made up my mind to fight him until I got a chance to jump out of the window. But I looked toward the bureau and saw an old fashioned pistol which you load from the muzzle and fired with a cap. My master was standing very close to this and the sight of it knocked all the manhood out of me, so I reluctantly pulled off my shirt with their assistance, and he tied my hands behind me, my feet together, and ran a stick between them. This left me in a doubled up position on the floor. He whipped and cursed me until he had cut my back to pieces. My mistress tried to take the whip from him, but he pushed her away so violently that once she fell on the floor. The second time she fell on the bed, but had secured the whip. He gave me a kick in my side, from which I have never recovered, and staggered from the room, being too drunk to whip me any more. His wife untied me and at the same time the old mother came to the door and said, "Master Scott, I came here to break this door open, for it's a shame for any woman's son to be cut up as you have done that child." He knocked the old lady down. I went up stairs and lay down on my stomach with my face across my arms. The next morning when I awoke the blood had dried the shirt in the wounds on my back. The cook had to grease the shirt so as to get it out of the wounds. Then he gave her medicine to heal my back. Every day after this when I would go to pile up wood I had to stoop my whole body, for my back was so sore that I couldn't bend it, and if I had not been so young (I was only eleven years,) the marks would have been visible until now, and like many other slaves, I would have carried them to judgment as a testimony against him.

After four or five weeks, when my back had become somewhat healed up, he told me one day if any one asked me if I had ever been whipped to tell them no. Is it not a wonder that negroes are not inveterate thieves and liars? They worked all the week for their masters, with only a peck of meal and three pounds of fat bacon, and after each day's labor they were compelled to go to their master's smoke house or chicken roost and steal enough to subsist upon the next day, to do that master's work, then, after this master had cut his back all to pieces he would compel him to tell a lie in order to sell him. But, thank God, we, like other nations, are born with the same natural instinct that others are, and although manhood was crushed for two hundred and forty odd years, yet, with the same surroundings and opportunities to develop them, we have risen above our environments.

One afternoon five negro traders came; my master called me, met me at the door, and repeated his former command "if any one asked me had I been whipped, to tell them no." I walked into the parlor; there sat five men wearing broad brimmed straw hats, their pants in their boots and a black snake whip across their shoulders. The first question they addressed to me was, had I ever been whipped. I suspect I was too slow in speaking, for the punishment had been too severe, and was too fresh in my memory for me to tell a lie on the spur of the moment. I had on a long straight gown which reached to my feet. The trader raised that and looked at my back and that told the story. They offered my master a small price for me, he refused it, and they left. I remained with him about three or four weeks longer, when one day he wrote a note and sent me to the trader's pen. The keeper, Mr. Howard, read it and told me to take it back to James, the negro turnkey, who also did all the whipping in the jail. He ordered me put in a cell and closed the big iron door, which told me that I was bound for Richmond, or some other slave market, and I was truly glad, for I now hated the soil upon which I was born.

I was in the trader's pen about three weeks. There were from one to ten slaves brought in every day. All of my brothers and sisters save two had been sold from Wilmington. Other slaveholders passing through had bought them, and it was said they were taken to Georgia. At the end of three weeks the gang of three hundred and fifty was made up and we were chained and started for Richmond, Virginia. In this gang was a woman named Fannie Woods. She had two children, the oldest about eight years, the other a nursing baby. She was not handcuffed as the others were, but tied above the elbow so she could shift the nursing baby in her arms. She led the older one by the hand. The first half of the day the little boy kept up pretty well; after that he became a hindrance in the march. The trader came back several times and ordered her to keep up. She told him she was doing the best she could. He threatened each time to whip her if she did not keep up, and finally he ordered a negro, a strong muscular man six feet in height, who went along to give us water and help drive, to untie her, made her give the baby to another woman, then ordered her to take off her waist. They buckled a strap around each wrist and strapped her to a large pine tree less than ten feet from the rest of us, and with a blacksnake whip the colored man was made to hit her fifty lashes on her bare back. The blood ran down as water but she never uttered a sound. She was ordered to put on her waist. They retied her and told her to see if they could keep up.

After going a few miles farther they sold the little boy she was leading to a man along the way. I heard the wails of the mother and the mourning of the other slaves on account of her sorrow, and heard the gruff voice of the trader as he ordered them to shut up. We marched until nine or ten o'clock, when we came to a boarding house that was kept especially for the accommodation of negro traders. This was a large log house of one room, about eighteen by twenty feet, with staples driven in all around the room and handcuffs attached to chains about four feet long. They would handcuff two or three slaves to each chain. In the summer they had nothing but the bare floor to lie upon; in the winter straw was put upon the floor. There was a very large fire place in this room.

We stopped at this boarding house. This was our first night's stop after leaving Wilmington. The keeper of the boarding house tried to buy Fannie Wood's baby, but there was a disagreement regarding the price. About five the next morning we started on. When we had gone about half a mile a colored boy came running down the road with a message from his master, and we were halted until his master came bringing a colored woman with him, and he bought the baby out of Fannie Woods' arms. As the colored woman was ordered to take it away I heard Fannie Woods cry, "Oh God, I would rather hear the clods fall on the coffin lid of my child than to hear its cries because it is taken from me." She said, "good bye, child." We were ordered to move on, and could hear the crying of the child in the distance as it was borne away by the other woman, and I could hear the deep sobs of a broken hearted mother. We could hear the groans of many as they prayed for God to have mercy upon us, and give us grace to endure the hard trials through which we must pass.

We marched all that day, and the second and third nights we stopped in the same kind of a place as the first night. They were buying and selling all along the way, so when we reached Richmond about ten o'clock the fourth night, there were about four hundred and fifty of us, footsore, hungry and broken-hearted.

CHAPTER VIII.

We were taken to Lee's negro traders' auction pen, which was a very large brick structure with a high brick wall all around it. A very large hall ran through the center. There was no furniture in it, not even a chair to sit upon. In this pen the handcuffs were taken off for the first time since we left home. There were possibly three or four hundred in there when we arrived. Many found relatives. One woman found her husband who had been sold from her three or four years before. But I was not so fortunate as to find any of my people.

The next morning the back door was open and we went down to wash. There were three or four pumps in the yard and long troughs near each. Some one would pump these troughs full of water and we would wash our faces and hands. There were no towels to wipe on, so some woman would give us her apron or dress skirt to dry our faces with. We then waited for our breakfast. The cooks handed out our tin pans with cabbage, or beans and corn bread, without knife, fork or spoon. Many having been sold before, and knowing how they would fare, carried such things with them. We sat around on the floor and ate our breakfast, after which we were ordered into a long hall, where we found wire cards, such as are used for wool, flax or hemp. We were ordered to comb our hair with them. Of course when we started we had on our best clothes, which consisted of a pair of hemp pants and cotton shirt; most of us were barefoot. The women, and sometimes the men, wore red cotton bandanas on their heads. After our toilets were completed we were ordered into a little ten by twelve room; we went in, ten or twelve at once. There were five or six young ladies in the gang I went in with. The traders, forgetting the sacredness of their own mothers and sisters, paid no respect to us, but compelled each one of us to undress, so as to see if we were sound and healthy. I heard Fannie Woods as she pleaded to be exempt from this exposure. They gave her to understand that they would have her hit one hundred lashes if she did not get her clothes off at once. She still refused, and when they tried to take them off by force, fought them until they finally let her alone.

From Log Cabin to the Pulpit; or, Fifteen Years in Slavery

After this humiliating ordeal of examination was over we went into the auction room. This was a large room about forty by sixty feet, with benches around the sides, where we were permitted to sit until our turn came to get on the auction block. The auctioneering began about nine o'clock each day and lasted until noon, began again at one o'clock and continued until five p. m. This was a perpetual business every day in the year, and the prices were quoted on the bulletin and in the papers the same as our stock and wheat are quoted today. At these sales we could find the best people of the South buying and selling.

I remember when I got on the block, the first bid was one hundred and fifty dollars. It went up to seven hundred, when the bidding ceased. The negro trader went to the auctioneer and told him that I came from the Madagascar tribe and that my father was an engineer and a skilled mechanic. Then the bidding became brief. I recall that the auctioneer said, "right and title guaranteed," as he slapped me on the head, then continued by saying "he's sound as a silver dollar." I was knocked off at eleven hundred and fifty dollars.

A poor man in East Virginia, named William Scott, bought me, paying four hundred and fifty dollars cash and giving a mortgage on his sixty acres of land, his stock and everything he owned, including one colored girl, whom he had bought four years before. The next morning after I was sold they brought a man to the traders' pen to he whipped. This man would not allow his overseer to whip him. He had chains on him that looked as though they were welded on. They took him upstairs in the big building where there were about seven or eight hundred men, women and children. It was about noon and they left him handcuffed while they went to dinner. He explained to us why they were about to whip him. He had gone to church without a pass on two occasions and refused to allow his master to whip him for so doing. His master declared he would whip him or kill him. They took the irons off, and ordered him to strip himself of all of his clothing. He promptly did so. His master said, "you might just as well have done this at home and you might have gotten off with a few hundred lashes." But to their surprise, when they told him to lie down, he began to knock men down right and left, with his feet and hands. Many went down before him. Then they picked out ten or twelve strong colored men, made them run in upon him, and though he knocked many of them down they were too many for him, so they overpowered him, and with straps fastened him taut upon the floor to six strong rings. These rings were arranged in two rows of three rings each, opposite each other and covering a space something over six feet in length.

Then his master, with four or five other men, came up to see him whipped, one man with his tally book, and a negro with his black snake whip and paddle; they brought their demijohn of whiskey, each one taking a drink before they began their bloody work. They even gave the negro who was compelled to do the whipping, a drink. After they were well drunk the whipping began. One man would count out until he counted nine, then with the tenth he would cry tally. When the whipping first began the slave would not say a word, but after awhile as they cut his back all to pieces, he would cry out, "pray, master," and in this way he pleaded for mercy until he grew so weak he could not utter a word. They gave him three hundred lashes, then washed his back with salt water and paddled it with a leather paddle about the size of a man's hand, with six holes in it. As they paddled him it sounded as a dead thud; you could hardly hear him grunt as each lick fell upon him. He was whipped from head to foot and the floor, where he was lying was a pool of blood when the brutal work was ended. His master congratulated the negro whipping master for the way he accomplished his part of the work, gave him another big drink of whiskey and ordered him to untie the man.

They all went down stairs and the other colored people who were in the room put the man's clothing on him. This was late in the afternoon. The next morning when I awoke I saw the men and women kneeling around in a circle, praying, groaning and crying. I walked up and looked to see what the trouble was, and I found the man they had whipped the day before cold in death. He was swollen so that his clothing had. bursted off. A jury of white men came up and held a mock inquest. I never heard what the verdict was. The colored men came with a mule cart, rolled him up in a sheet and took him to his last resting place.

I stayed in this trader's pen three days after my new master bought me, and during this time I saw hundreds of mothers separated from their children. I heard the wail of many a child for its mother, and of the mother for her child. While one buyer had the mother, going in one direction, another with the child would be going the opposite way. I saw husband and wife bidding each other farewell and sisters and brothers being separated. There could not have been any darker days to them than these; it was with them as it was with Job, when he spake in the Third Chapter of Job, and said:

"Let the day perish wherein I was born, and the night in which it is said there is a man child conceived, let that day be darkness; let not God regard it from above, neither let the light shine upon it."

"Let darkness and the shadow of death stain it; let a cloud dwell upon it, let the blackness of the day terrify it. As for that night, let darkness seize upon it; let it not be joined unto the days of the year, let it not come into the number of the months. Lo, let that night be solitary, let no joyful voice come therein. Let them curse it that curse the day, who are ready to raise up their mourning. Let the stars of the twilight thereof be dark; let it look for light, but have none, neither let it see the dawning of the day; because it shut not up the doors of my mother's womb, nor hid sorrow from mine eyes."

These were the lamentations of the poor slaves, but still they prayed for the dawn and light of a better day. Like Israel, many looked long and eagerly for freedom but died without the sight. Thank God, over three million lived to see the sunlight in all its brilliancy, and we can now look back and say: "The Lord has done great things for us, whereof we are glad."

CHAPTER IX.

On the fourth morning after I was sold, I got on the horse behind my new master. I had a handcuff on my right wrist, with a chain extending down to my right foot and locked around my ankle. We rode until late in the afternoon, when we stopped at a hotel. He chained me to the porch and left me until after supper time; then gave me a piece of bread and meat, and left me until about ten o'clock at night, while he talked. Then he came after me and we went up stairs to his room. He chained me to his bed post, and gave me a quilt to lie on by the side of his bed, on the floor.

The next morning we had breakfast by daylight and started again on our journey; to my surprise he didn't handcuff me this time. He talked very freely with me, told me he had a nice girl and if I acted all right we would have a good time, and he would soon buy my mother and father, when the poor fellow was not able to buy me; he had just finished paying the mortgage which he gave when he bought the girl, and remortgaged to buy me. About nine o'clock the succeeding night we arrived home; when quite a distance from the house he called out in a loud voice for Fanny to open the gate. As we neared the gate, she threw it open. I had ridden until my limbs would not hold me up when I slid off the horse, so I fell prostrate upon the ground, but with the assistance of the girl and my master, I was able to get on my feet.

His residence was a large log building of one room. He left me at the door and told me to stay there until he called me. Now, it was a custom with my people, when a white man went on the inside and closed the door and left a black man, woman or child outside, just so sure a black ear went to the key hole. I didn't want to make an exception to this rule, so when he went in, my ear went to the key hole. After the usual mode of family greeting of a man that had been away from home a week or ten days, he said: "The one who guesses what I have brought, may have it." The oldest boy said, "A pair of boots, for you promised me a pair;" the nine-year-old girl said, "A large china doll," but when the guessing came to the smallest one, a little girl between the age of three and four years, to my surprise she said, "A nigger." "Correct," said my master, "the rigger's yours; come in here, Bill" I went in and the formal introduction was made He said, beginning with the boy, "This is your master Charles, this is your Miss Mary," but when it came to the youngest girl, he said, this is your Miss Alice and you belong to her. Now, if you are a good and obedient nigger, when she is grown and at her death she will set you free." If I had believed this story I would have prayed to God to kill her then, wicked as it was. Then he gave me an introduction to his wife. As long as I had been with him he had not introduced himself until now. He really grew enthusiastic in introducing himself; his face grew red, and his voice trembled as he said: "I want you to understand that I'm a nigger breaker. I hear you came from a family of niggers that won't be whipped, but I'll break you or kill you." I knew he could not afford to do the latter, for I had overheard Robert E. Lee, from whom he had bought me, say to him. "I understand you have abused the girl you bought from me, shamefully. If you abuse this boy it will cost you all you are worth."

He then called the girl, who was once a pretty octoroon, but now her face was much disfigured where the mistress had stuck the hot tongs to it because she was so overworked she would fall asleep while she would be carding wool at night. You could hardly see the traces of a once beautiful girl, now about fourteen years old.

He said, "you two have got a good home and can be happy here together." Jokingly, he said, "I'll have the preacher come over and marry you." He thought through this union - he had formed in his mind - that he would raise his own slaves.

After supper the mistress ordered her to bring in her tin pan and quart cup, at the same time wondering what dishes to give me to use. My master said. "Oh yes, I forgot to tell you I bought Bill a new pan and cup." The children scampered away for the old saddle bags. They brought my cup and pan, and after using the latter for a looking glass for a time, handed it to me. In the tin pans she put a little gravy and a corn dodger on each, and filled the cups with skimmed milk - the milk had been skimmed and skimmed until there was not an eye of cream to be seen on it. We called it blue John. Fannie and I went into the kitchen She said to me, "don't eat yet, we'll milk first." I was very hungry, but did as she asked me. We took our milk buckets and went to the cow pen; there were two cows, so we got them close together. Fannie milked both, for I had never before tried to milk. We poured our cup of blue John into the milk pail. She milked both our cups full, and with our hoe cakes of corn bread, we ate our supper, drinking the warm, unstrained milk. The mistress often complained, and spoke of selling the cows because tbey gave such poor milk. We would then milk the cows into the pail where we had poured our skimmed milk and return it to our mistress. We continued this as long as I was there, which was three or four months.

My master was overseer for a man on an adjoining farm, named Howard, for which he was paid thirty dollars per month. He would leave home at three o'clock in the morning, giving the girl and me our task the night before. He would eat his dinner each day in the field with the slaves, and return home at about nine or ten o'clock at night. He hired the slaves at night, and sometimes in the day he would slip them over to work in his crop. I have known the slaves many times to work in his field from ten o'clock at night until near day-break the next morning; yet he never allowed the girl or me to visit the slaves on any other farm, or them to visit us. He was the meanest overseer in that section of the country, for he would have a whipping bee every Monday morning.

He had whipping posts on the farm and the slaves were tied to this and whipped; you could hear the cries of slaves all around from that place. I have heard him laugh many times and tell how the slaves would squirm under the lash.

The farm on the other side of us belonged to a man named Wilkerson; he had seventy five or a hundred slaves, and he, also, was a cruel man. Every day, in going for the cows I would have to pass his farm. I heard him say to one of the rail splitters, "if you don't have your task of rails split tomorrow I will hit you one hundred lashes." The man told him he was doing all he could do and would die before he would take a single lick. I made it my business the next day to go after the cows about the time for him to go out; I saw him and four or five other men; he asked the rail splitter if he had his task completed. The man answered in the negative; he then ordered him to pull off his shirt, which the man did, then tied his pants around his waist with his suspenders. The reason the slaves would so readily pull off their shirts was so they could not have anything to hold them by, their flesh being moist they could not easily hold them. When his master told him to cross his hands he began to fight, knocking white men down as fast as they could come to him. Finally they made five or six other rail splitters, working near by, help take him. There were saw logs from five to six feet through, all round; some of the colored men caught him by the head and hands, while others had hold of his feet, and they bent him back over one of the saw-logs while he was fighting and cursing. His master seized the maul, which the man had been using to split rails with, and struck him across the abdomen; bent over in the position he was the lick sounded like a pop-gun, and the man's intestines ran out, and he died across the log; murdered because he could not perform the task imposed upon him. These are some of the horrible deeds which have stained the pages of American history, and which it will take centuries to mitigate.

It was a common thing to hear the cries of the slaves all around on Monday morning. Some being whipped for one thing, some for another. Some were whipped for attending religious services on Sunday; some for going to frolics; sometimes a man's wife was owned by other masters five or six miles away; they would slip-off after their work was done at night to see them; sometimes they would be late returning, so they would be whipped for that. There would be a perfect pandemonium around that community all the time.

CHAPTER X.

I would often talk to Fannie about running away; she would plead with me and beg me not to, because it would be so lonesome for her, but there was a constant yearning in my soul for that freedom which God intended for all human beings. Ultimately, after a careful planning of the route to be taken and a survey of the country, as far as I had been over, I made up my mind to leave. One morning my master sent me to the field to gather corn. I carried a basket and two sacks, and at noon I was to fill them and hitch up the mule cart and bring them home. I got the corn ready and sat down in the corn row. I realized then for the first time that there must be some efficacy in prayer. My mother had taught me to get on my knees and say my prayers, as far back as I could remember, yet I never knew the power there was in prayer, until on this memorable morning, I knelt down in a corn row and prayed with that fervent, childlike simplicity for God in some way to get me hack to my mother or into Canada, or else let me die and go to heaven. The Queen of England had said that if the slaves could reach the shores of Canada she would protect them, if it took the whole navy of England to do so. While I was thus in prayer it seemed that all nature was in sympathy with me, for not even the rustling of the leaves could be heard. The only thing to break the monotony was the wooing of a turtle dove that sat in the branches of a distant tree, and seemed to he saying to me, "I am in deep sympathy with you." Reasoning came to me as audibly as though some one was speaking to me, saying "you shall see your mother again."

I became so much elated over this message, though received from an unseen power, that I jumped up and at once fully decided what course to take. Immediately I proceeded to put my decision into action, so I emptied the corn out of the two sacks and the basket; put the sacks in the basket on my arm and left that corn field with the full intention of going back to Richmond, Virginia.

It may seem strange to the reader that I would go back to this place of human misery; but I had learned from older men and women who had been sold to some poor man, that if they would run away and go back to their former master, and tell him "that your master was so mean that you could not live with him, and for this reason you had run away and come back to him," nine times out of ten he would accept this piece of deception practiced by the slave, and compel the poor man to take his money back, believing that the negro thought more of him than of the man he had sold him to, and for this reason I was going back to Richmond, Virginia.

I went about seven or eight miles that day through the woods, and about dusk I came in sight of a cabin in the distance. I was satisfied this was the home of some old mother or father who had outlived the days of their usefulness, and was given a peck of meal each week and cast off to fish or hunt for the rest of their living. I was not disappointed, for I found an old woman eighty years old; it was hard to discover until she spoke whether she was white or slave. The first words the old lady said were, "Son, you is a runaway, aint you? I told her that I was, and she told me "the overseer haven't been around yet cause dey aint done milking yit, but you take this path (as she pointed to a path) and follow it till you come to a log across de creek, with a fish box upon it; you sit there until you hear me singing this song, God has delivered Daniel, and why not deliver me?" She went into the house, while I went to the log mentioned. I sat there for three-quarters of an hour. I heard the milk maids while milking singing different melodies, then I heard the command of the overseer for them to take the cows to pasture, and in a short while I heard the feeble voice of the old mother as it rang out on the still, balmy air, singing:

He delivered Daniel from the lion's den,
Jonah from the body of the whale,
The Hebrew children from the fiery furnace,
And why not deliver poor me?

Hold up your head with courage bold,
And do not be afraid;
For my God delivered Daniel,
And He will deliver poor you.

I started for the house and met her coming. We went into the cabin where she had prepared supper, and I assure you I enjoyed it. The supper consisted of boiled fresh fish and "ash cake." As I ate she sat with her hands on my head, telling me how to get along in the world, and pointing me to that friend that sticketh closer than a brother. She repeatedly said, "if God be for you it is more than all the world against you." She made me a pallet upon the floor, and I slept there until about three-thirty o'clock the next morning, when she awoke me and gave me breakfast of the same diet I had had the night previous for supper. She also gave me four or five onions, and told me upon the peril of my life, not to eat a single one of these onions, because they would make me sleepy and I would be liable to be caught. But she said negro hunters came along there every two or three hours in the day; and I learned for the first time how to decoy the blood hounds, for she told me whenever I heard the baying of hounds on my trail, to rub the onions on the bottoms of my feet and run, and after running a certain distance to stop and apply the onions again, then when I came to a large bushy tree, to rub the trunk as high up as I could reach, then climb the tree.

CHAPTER XI.

About four o'clock in the morning, at the old woman's command, I knelt by her side, she placed her hand upon my head and prayed fervently for my safe return to Richmond, and that God would touch Massa Lee's heart, that he might buy me back from my present owner. When she quit praying she told me that I would reach Richmond safely. She kissed me good bye, with tender, parting words, as a mother would her own son, and I left, with directions from her how to reach my intended destination. I had not gone far when an opportunity presented itself to test the efficacy of the onions, for about nine o'clock that day I heard the baying of the blood hounds in the distance behind me. I rubbed the onions on my feet as directed, and ran as fast as I could the distance of half a mile, when I repeated the application. I continued this process for about one mile and a half, going across the fields and through the woods, dodging the roads and farms where people were at work. I came to a thickly branched out tree in the woods. I rubbed onions on the trunk and climbed the tree. I could tell when the hounds came to the place where I first put the onions on my feet, because they would retrace their steps, until finally their voices died away, and I heard them no more that day. I traveled all of that day, and that night I slept in a low, swampy place between two huge logs, on some brush, with the two sacks over me which I took when I left the corn field. By daylight the next morning I started on my journey, but had not gone many miles when I came in sight of a river. I saw that I was not far from a house, and went close enough to see that a ford was near the house where they crossed the river. The white man who had charge of the ford lived in the house. So I knew I couldn't get across the river without taking a boat, and that he wouldn't hire me one without word from my master, therefore that necessitated my waiting until night, so I went back in the woods to wait.

I saw some colored men coming across the field and went to meet them, and learned through them their master's name and three or four slaves that he owned, and name of a farmer on the other side of the river. They told me to go to the ferryman and tell him that Mr.

Howard, my master, had sent me to take the basket and two sacks to Mr. Owens, who lived on the other side of the river. They told me that the ferryman would question me very minutely, but if he asked how long Mr. Howard had owned me to tell him he bought me from negro traders two weeks before - for traders had crossed there just two weeks ago with three or four hundred slaves. They then left me and told me to wait until they returned. I did so, but under great suspense, because one of the men belonged to a tribe of negroes known as the Guineas, who would divulge any secret for a little whiskey or wheat bread; therefore I was afraid I would be betrayed. But in a short time they returned, relieving me of the great suspense, and bringing me something to eat. They told me I was in an easy day's walk of Richmond after I crossed the river; told me what to say to Massa Lee when I got back, but not to go into Richmond until after dark. They prayed an ardent prayer for God's protection and guiding hand to go with me, and bade me good bye and God speed. I went to the ford, called out hello; the harsh voice of the ferryman cried out, "whose thar." At the same time he was coming towards the river, I was fast rehearsing in my mind the story I was to tell him. When he got near me his first words were, "where in hell are you going this time of night?" I started to tell him that Mr. Howard had sent me to Mr. Owen's to take the basket and sacks, but before I could finish telling him, he ordered me to pull off my hat: that he would teach me some manners if I came there talking to him with my hat on. He then asked how long Mr. Howard had owned me, at the same time flashing his lantern in my face. But when I told him he said, "yes, I remember seeing you in that gang; untie the boat." He sat down and lit his pipe while I pulled the boat over. When we reached the other side he said "tie her up thar." He looked at his watch and said "its a quarter up thar and a quarter back." I'll give you fifteen minutes each way, if you sent back in that time I'll skin you alive." If he's waiting he is having a good long wait. I went on my way rejoicing and saying, as the little colored boy said who had been accustomed to climbing the ladder and sleeping in one of his mistress's bed rooms when his master was not at home. But one memorable night when he got to the bed he found old master was there, so he said. "may I, old master, may I?" Master said, "may you what, you black rascal, you." Sambo as quick as lightning, said, "may I feed the little pigs with the big ones?" With an oath his master told him yes; for him to get out of there. Sambo was so much elated over his success that he said, as he started down the ladder, "wasn't dat well turned?" The master hearing him, inquired "what's that well turned?"

Sambo was ready again with an answer. He said, "my foot slipped and I fell twice around de ladder and cotched myself and didn't fall yit."

After crossing the river that night I went but a short distance, when I made me a bed in a shock of fodder. The next morning before daylight as I came out of the shock two more runaways came out of the shock ahead of me. When they saw me they ran as fast as they could go and I after them. They did not wait to see whether I was white or black. They ran across a large field, and came to a fence. One, a very tall man, put his hand on the top and vaulted over. The other one attempted to follow but fell back. By that time I had caught up with him. He asked me why I did not tell him I was colored. I replied, "I couldn't cotch you."

They were men who had been sold from Richmond and were now running away from their masters as I was, and trying to get back to Lee. They had with them plenty to eat, so we had about as good a time that day as runaways could have in the woods. Long before dusk we could see the statue of George Washington, which stood at Richmond, Virginia, with a negro boy chained at its base, and Washington pointing with his right hand, saying, "take the negro south." This very great man, who, with Hancock, in 1776, signed the Declaration of Independence, and said the colonies were and ought to be free, loosed them from the iron hand of Great Britain; and yet that was the inscription written on his statue, which adorned the public square of the once Capitol of the Southern Confederacy.

We hid around until dusk, when we went down to a spring and ate our lunch slaking our thirst from the clear cool water as it bubbled out from the spring, by lying flat down and lapping the water. I happened to be the first of the three to get up, and to my surprise there stood five negro hunters with their guns and revolvers pointing toward us. I said to my companions "here is some white men." They said "whar." Their eyes looked like great balls of cotton. The men commanded us to come to them. I can best illustrate how we appeared when we found out that we had been captured, by a cartoon which I once saw. The cartoon represented an old colored man who saw an opossum in a tree close to his house; he was so elated over the idea of possum and sweet potatoes that he climbed the tree. The possum jumped upon the limb the man was on, but it got between him and the trunk of the tree; the old man had his saw and began in earnest to saw the limb off, thinking of nothing but the possum; he said to his boy and dog below, "look out down dar, cause sumphin gwine to drap." And "something did drap," but it was the old man himself. Likewise, when we three looked up into the muzzles of the guns and revolvers we thought something was going to drop, and sure enough something did, for we dropped, each one of us in handcuffs, and we were marched into Richmond.

S. J. RICHARDSON,
Editor Bedford, Ind., Enterprise, who has given valuable assistance and friendship to the author.

CHAPTER XII.

When we arrived at the negro trader's pen, Mr Lee happened to be there. He wanted to know of the negro hunters where they found us; they told him. Then he began to interrogate each of us; I told him that "Massa Scott was so mean to me that I could not live with him, so I ran off and came back to you." The other two men told the same kind of story; so Mr. Lee ordered the negro hunters to take the handcuffs off, and if they wanted to make money to go and find negroes that were not coming back to him. They, with their hats in their hands, the same as the slaves, began to form excuses, when Lee ordered them off the premises without any reward. Had we not been returning to Mr. Lee they would have been entitled to three dollars per head. According to the law they were entitled to it at any rate, for we were runaways, but they were poor men with low occupations and their word didn't go as far as that of the slaves they were driving. One of the men he ordered locked up stairs, telling him that he had a good master, and if he behaved himself he would he treated all right. The man begged very hard not to be sent back, but his begging was all in vain. This man's master was wealthy, while mine and the other man's master were poor men, so he kept us and sent the other man back.

Mr. Lee told me that the man who had my mother had been there twice and wanted to buy me, and Scott, he said "was behind anyhow." I think he meant that his second payment was overdue- - and he assured me that he shouldn't have me back. Mr. Lee wrote a note and sent me to his own house. I met an old colored mammy at the gate. She asked me, "where is you gwine?" I said, "to see Miss Lee." She said, "You look like gwine to see Miss Lee. Wha dat you got in your han?" I said, "a letter for her." She said, "gin it to me." She took the note, telling me to wait. Mrs. Lee raised the window and called me to come up. She asked about my parents, and said Mr. Scott should not take me back again. She told the colored mammy to take me and clean me up. When I got in the cabin I discovered it was wash day, for she had a kettle of hot water on the fire place. She took a couple of handfuls of soft soap out of the gourd and stirred it in the water. When she found I was not undressing she looked very much surprised and said, "gwine out of dem rags." She scrubbed my back till my flesh burned. About the time she was through the sixteen-year old maid came in with clothing for me. I tried to hide behind the old mother. The girl threw the clothes down and ran out. I put the clothes on and stayed at the trader's pen that evening. After that I was privileged to stay at the house, or pen, as I chose. I thought I was almost a free man, for I had on a pair of shoes, a nice suit of clothes and a large brass watch and chain.

Master Lee told me that a man named Jake Hadley, who lived in Greenville, Tennessee, had my mother, two brothers and a sister. He also said Mr. Hadley drove a big black horse so it seems that I thought there was only one black horse in all Virginia and that the Jew owned him; therefore I met with many disappointments. I waited and watched for more than a month for my new master to come, during which time I assisted Peter around the pen. Peter looked after the slaves, and did all the whipping. I cleaned the office and was errand boy. Most of my work was about the office. During the time I was there I saw thousands of slaves bought and sold. I saw one woman who had five children; she and two children, one a nursing baby, and a girl about eleven years old, were sold to negro traders, while the husband and the other three children were bought by a farmer who lived somewhere in east Virginia. The farmer went with the father and three children to see the mother and the other two children leave for Mississippi. As the boat pulled out from the shore and the husband and wife bade each other good bye, the woman, with one loud scream, made a sudden leap and landed in the deep water, with her baby clasped in her arms and the little girl handcuffed to her. She had preferred death to life separated from her husband and children. They were not picked up until the next day.

I saw another woman whipped seventy-five lashes on her bare back because she wouldn't strip her clothing any further down than her waist, to be examined. They took her back the second time, but she fought them until they were compelled to leave her alone. These last two incidents remind me of the pilgrim in the following song:

From Log Cabin to the Pulpit; or, Fifteen Years in Slavery

"I saw a blood washed traveler in garments white assnow,
While traveling up the highway, where heavenly breezes blow;
His path was full of trials, but yet his face was bright,
He shouted as he journeyed, I'm glad the burden's light.

CHORUS.

Then it's palms of victory,
Crowns of glory,
Palms of victory, you shall wear.

I saw him 'mong his neighbors, they mocked his soul's alarm;
The vilest wretch among them could scoff and do no harm;
Forsaken by his kindred and banished from their sight,
An outcast, yet he shouted, I'm glad the burden's light.

I saw him in the conflict, where all around was strife,
Where wicked men with malice, connived to take his life;
I saw him cast in prison, a dungeon dark as night,
And there I heard him shouting, I'm glad the burden's light.

I saw him led from prison, and chained unto the stake,
I heard him cry triumphant, 'tis all for Jesus sake.
I saw the fires when kindled, the faggots burning bright,
He said the yoke is easy, the burden is so light."

CHAPTER XIII.

This is now the year of 1860. I was twelve years of age and had been a runaway twice in that time. I had now been at Lee's trader's pen four or five weeks, when one day I saw a man coming with a black horse and buggy; something from within seemed to whisper to me, "this is the man who owns your mother." My aspirations ran so high that I went out the back way and prayed that this might be he. He came into the office of the pen, and after a general conversation with Mr. Lee, he asked "if he had heard anything of that boy yet." I was watching every move and listening to every word passed. With a wink of the eye, Mr. Lee said, "no." Then he sent me to do something in the rear end of the building. I did it very quickly and returned to the office again; was very busily engaged with my dust brush. Never since I had been there had I found so much to be done in the office, and whenever I was sent away I would do my errand as quickly as possible and return to the office again.

Finally Mr. Hadley, for it was he, said: "boy, how would you like to belong to me and go down to Tennessee to live? While I was satisfied that he was the man who owned my mother, I said, "I wouldn't like to go with you at all, 'cause Massa Lee said the man that had my mother was coming after me." As I spoke I couldn't keep from crying, and Mr. Lee could refrain no longer, so he said "William, this is Mr. Hadley, the man who has your mother, and brothers and sisters." And for once I saw that seemingly heartless man, who separated thousands of husbands and wives, mothers and children, sisters and brothers, touched to the very core, for he drew his handkerchief and wiped his eyes, instead of his nose, as he pretended to be doing.

Mr. Hadley was a very kind, fatherly acting man. He bought me a nice suit of clothes, and gave me money, telling me to buy my mother, brothers and sisters some presents. As a general thing all Jew slave owners were more lenient to their slaves than any other nationality, perhaps because they had been in bondage themselves. In a few days we started for home; we had to stop along the way in many little towns to attend to business, so that we were nearly four days in making the trip. These were four of the longest days I had ever experienced in my life, for I was anxious to meet my mother again. I was constantly inquiring "how much farther is it." On the fourth day in the afternoon I asked, "how long yet before we will reach home?" He said, "in a few days now." The words had scarcely left his lips, when I saw coming down the road my mother and new mistress. Mother came upon the side of the buggy my master was on, and almost dragged me out of the buggy across my master. She was rejoicing and blessing master for his deeds of kindness. In a few minutes my new mistress came up on the other side of the buggy; she pulled me over, and to my surprise, and for the first time in my life, a white woman kissed me. This was a very new feature to me, and naturally embarrased me very much, so much so that I mentioned it many times afterwards. I couldn't understand how it was, I, a slave, and she my mistress, as others had been, and they were so heartless and cruel, and she so kind. But I afterwards learned that all the white people were not mean and cruel, for when I arrived home I found my mistress had prepared a grand dinner for us and invited in all the slaves. My mistress had two children, Samuel and Laura. I didn't call them master and mistress as I had heretofore called the white children, but called them each by their given name. I had a glorious time in that home and felt almost as if I were free. My master owned a large farm three miles from Greenville, where we lived. But during the month of February he concluded to go to the old country- - I think it was on account of the agitation of the slave question - he saw the war was coming on, so he decided to take us back to Wilmington and leave us there, with his wife and children, on his brother's farm, until he returned. Accordingly we all packed up and went back to Wilmington, N. C., my old birthplace. On arriving there we found another brother and sister, making mother and six children together again; father and the other six children we knew nothing of. Mr. Hadley went away but was gone only three weeks, when he returned, saying he had not gone any farther than Richmond, Virginia.

He stayed in Wilmington a month, and when he was ready to go back home he asked me and my sister "if we didn't want to stay with his brother awhile longer and come home later on." We, not having the least suspicion that he had sold us, told him that we would. So they went home, leaving us. After a couple of weeks, Mr. Dave Hadley - that was his brother's name - told us that he had bought us, but we could go every two or three months to Greenville to see mother.

It was not more than two weeks from the time I found that Massa Dave Hadley had bought me, when Joseph Cowens, the son of my original old master, came to Mr. Hadley's; he met me out in the yard and stopped me for a talk. He said, "it was a shame that his father had allowed my father to be sold away, that he was going to buy us all back and get us together again."

With this conversation he naturally won me, so when he asked me if I wouldn't like to belong to him, of course I said "yes." He went into the house and in a short time be and Massa Dave came out together, and Massa Dave told me that I now belonged to Joseph Cowens, and that he bad bought my two brothers also, and in the next two months he was going to buy mother and the other two children. But when I got to his house and asked for my brothers, he said that he had hired them out for a year. I soon found out different; he had never bought my brothers, nor had any intention of buying them; or my mother, either.

CHAPTER XIV.

I am now back in the Cowens family, my original master's son, and brother to Scott Cowens - the man I knocked off the porch for hitting my mother, and who was afterwards drowned. I went to Joseph Cowen's as general servant boy in the house, and was treated as well as could be expected from a Cowen. I stayed there quite satisfied, thinking that mother and the other children would come in a few months, as he had promised they would. The last of March we moved out on the Summer farm, three miles from town, and I had to drive him to town every morning and go for him every evening. He was a merchant and owned several ships. Now I had a great deal of freedom out on the farm, for I did nothing but drive Massa Joseph back and forth, to and from town, and wait table. I was in the cabins and among the slaves the most of my time in the day, but I slept at the "great house" in Massa Joseph's room. I had become almost a prophet among my people, because I would get the news from the white people, and in the day would tell it to the slaves in the fields and cabins.

He owned another farm five miles from town, and had a colored overseer on this farm. Uncle Tom was the meanest man you ever saw, in the presence of the white folks. He would draw back his whip as though he was going to knock down all around him, but I never knew him to strike an old person in my life.

The leading white men from town would come out two or three nights in a week and stay half of the night and gamble. I would take the whiskey, glasses and water in to them, then Massa Joe would send me off to bed, but I stood many an hour listening to them talk and discuss the question of the war, and whether it would be advisable to arm the negroes. They finally decided, as did the Egyptians, that if they did arm the negroes when the enemy came the slaves would join with the enemy and fight against them, so they thought it would not be expedient to do so. About this time, or in February, 1861, delegates from South Carolina, Alabama, Georgia, Louisana and Texas, met at Montgomery, Alabama, and formed a government called the Confederate States of America. Jefferson Davis, of Mississippi, was chosen president. Davis came to Wilmington and was given a great ovation, and in his speech he appealed very strongly to the ladies; he asked, "which lady there was not willing to give her husband, son, brother or sweetheart, to go upon the battle field and fight for their rights." The women became frantic with their cries, "I will give mine," "I wouldn't marry a man who wouldn't go," etc. Then he made another appeal to the ladies, asking "which one of them would like to live to see the day when a nigger wench would be on equality with them?" At this point they grew raving mad, ante cried, "they never wanted to see that day." Jeff said he would wade in blood to his saddle skirts rather than live to see that day, and yet he tried to escape in his wife's skirts.

About this time the laws were very strict on the slaves, and they were not allowed a pass to go to a public gathering of any kind. Men who belonged to one man and whose wives were owned by another, and had been given a pass every Saturday night to go to see them, were now permitted to go only once a month. But the slaves would slip off to church and frolics and the patrollers were continually after them, but the slaves would play all kinds of tricks on them. I remember one time while at a prayer meeting in an old deserted cabin on the back part of a farm the slaves were singing and praying, but had several stationed all around the house, watching. They saw the patrollers coming and notified those in the house, and to my surprise five or six men had shovels, and each man got a shovel full of hot embers out of the fireplace and stood at the door and windows. They continued to sing and pray until the patrollers got to the door and ordered it opened. One man snatched the door open while the others threw the fire all over them; when the patrollers recovered consciousness the slaves were all gone.

At another time I went to a dance in the woods; the music consisted of tambourine, banjo and bones, but before the dance began they tied grapevines across the road, just high enough to catch a man riding horse back across the face or neck. When they heard the patrollers coming they ran, and the patrollers right after them; many of them were crippled, but not a slave was hurt or caught, So you see, there were some negro as well as Yankee tricks.

The slaves would have to devise many schemes in order to serve God. Of course they had church once or twice a month, but some white man would do the preaching, and his text would always be, "Servants obey your masters," But this was not what our people wanted to hear, so they would congregate after the white people had retired, when you would see them with their cooking utensils, pots and kettles, go into a swamp and put the pots and kettles on the fence, with the mouths turned toward the worshipers. They would sing and pray, the kettles catching the sound. In this way they were not detected. I did not learn until just before the war why they carried the vessels with them to worship.

In order to notify the slaves on other farms when there was going to be a meeting they would sing this song, and the slaves would understand what it meant. White people would think they were only singing for amusement:

"Get you ready, there's a meeting here tonight." Matt. 7: 16.

1 Get you ready, there's a meeting here tonight,
Come along there's a meeting here tonight,
I know you by your daily walk,
There's a meeting here tonight.

2 Oh, hallelujah, to the lamb,
There's a meeting here tonight,
For the Lord is on the given hand,
There's a meeting here tonight.

3 If ever I reach the mountain top,
I'll praise my Lord and never stop,
Get you ready, there's a meeting here tonight.

4 Go down to the river when you're dry
And there you'll get your full supply,
Get ready, there's a meeting here tonight.

5 You may hinder me here,
But you cannot there,
God sits in heaven
And he answers prayer.
There's a meeting here tonight.

They would carry with them iron lamps, with a greasy rag for a wick, and they would attach a sharp spike to the lamp so as to stick it in a tree. In this way they would light up the swamp, while they held their meeting.

CHAPTER XV.

SLAVE HOLDERS' CONSISTENT FAMILY WORSHIP

THE SLAVE HOLDERS' MORNING SERVICE.

SLAVEOWNERS' WORSHIP.

Air - any long metre.

"Come let us join, our God to praise,
Who lengthens out our fleeting days.
The shades of one more night have passed
Which has to many been the last.

And thus, Kind Providence, it seems,
Has kept us through our midnight dreams.
Our dogs have guarded well the door
And Lord, what could we ask Thee more?

Thy promise, Lord, has been our stay;
Not e'en a slave has run away,
While scores have left on every side
To seek Lake Erie's doleful tide.

O! grant us, Lord, a great display
Of Thy rich mercies through this day.
May we in strength our work pursue,
And love Thee as slave-holders do."

Let us unite in prayer:

"Supremely great, and worthy of all adoration art Thou, O Lord, our
heavenly Father. The cattle upon a thousand hills, and the negroes in
a thousand fields are Thine. We thank Thee, Lord, for the manifold
blessings with which Thou art supplying us, Thine humble and
obedient servants, notwithstanding our merits deserve them all, for

Thou hast said the righteous shall enjoy the good of the land. Now, Lord, we have not much time to pray, for Thou see'st how those devilish slaves are squandering away their time. Lord, revive Thy work in our midst. Grant us all a large increase of slaves for the traders this fall, that we may obtain the means, through Thy well directed providence, to rear Thee a magnificent temple in which Thou wilt love to dwell, and where Thou wilt love to pour out Thy spirit upon Thy Zion. O! Lord God, when we go into the fields among those ignorant, hard headed creatures, (over whom Thou hast made us to rule), may Thy glory so shine in our countenances that one of us shall subdue a thousand, and bind ten thousand upon the racks from the ungovernable malice of enraged negroes. Deliver us from the influence of a guilty conscience; deliver us from the abolition creeds, and from the slanderous tongues of enthusiastic politicians. Deliver us from insurrections and perplexity of minds, good Lord, deliver us. Give us and our dogs our daily bread, and our negroes their full pecks of parched corn or cotton seeds per week. Strengthen the horse and his rider, and make the limbs of the fugitive weak. Confound the cunning schemes of anti-slavery men. Bless the government which Thou didst redeem from the British yoke of oppression, and didst wash and make clean by the precious blood of the heroes of '76. Bless the star spangled banner, which floats over the land of the free and the home of the brave. May her stars increase in number and brightness, and eagle's wings be extended o'er all the virgin soil of our continent until his beak shall pick the fugitive from his lurking places in the cold regions of British America, while his tail shall overshadow the slaves in Yucatan. And may his pinions cast their pleasant shade over all the free born sons of America, from Providence to Monterey, while he shall bear in his mighty talons, for ages to come, four millions of ignorant slaves with all their posterity. Hear us, good Lord, and according to Thy manifold mercies, bless and sanctify us. Give us more than we are able to ask for at this time, and in the end save all the white people who have supported Thy holy institution and performed Thy will, through Jesus Christ, our Redeemer, Amen."

SLAVE HOLDERS' CONSISTENT FAMILY WORSHIP.

THE SLAVE HOLDERS' HYMN TO BE SUNG AT
EVENING PRAYERS. (Short Metre.)

"A charge to keep I have,
A negro to maintain.
Help me, O Lord, whilst here I live,
To keep him bound in chain.
We thank Thee, Lord, for grace
That's brought us safe this far,
 While many of our dying race
Were summoned to Thy bar.

No negroes have I lost -
Not one has run away.
I have been faithful to my trust
Through this, another day.
Lord, we cannot lie down
Till we implore Thy grace,
For if we do a mighty frown
Will cover o'er Thy face.

Draw nigh, just now, O Lord,
And listen while we pray,
And each petition - every word,
Pray Answer and Obey.

SLAVE-HOLDERS' CONSISTENT SERMON.

Copied from imagination's parchment roll, where this, and many
other things, have been on perpetual record from childhood.
Ficticious, as it is, and as ridiculous as it may appear, I defy any
minister, white or black, who preaches to the slaves in the south, to
preach any better doctrines and have his preaching harmonize with
the institution of slavery. The whole sentiment is consistent with

slavery, and the old experienced southerner will read many things in this discourse which he has heard before. This is preached more generally on the Sabbath, previous to the usual holidays by the "Rt. Rev. Bishop Policy."

"Well, darkies, I am happy to see so many shining eyes, and greasy faces today. It speaks two great truths; first, that you are all awake to your own welfare; and secondly, that your masters treated you well and gave you meat. You have come out today to hear the word of God. I hope you will pay strict attention to what is said, and treasure it up in good and honest hearts. My text is not taken directly from the Bible, that is, not our Bible, but yours. We all respect your Bible more than we do the white man's Bible, or otherwise the word of God, for your Bible you can obey, but ours you cannot. The text is recorded in the laws of Maryland, A. D. 1715, Chapter 44, Section 22. "All negroes and other slaves already imported, or hereafter to be imported into this province, and all children born, or hereafter to be born of such negroes and slaves, shall be slaves during their natural lives." In the first place, I shall show God's wisdom displayed in the system of slavery. Second, the master's great responsibility. Third and last, the consequence of disobedience. God's wisdom is displayed in the system of slavery. The text declares positively that you shall all be slaves during your natural lives. What a great blessing God has brought to you, my colored friends, through the economy of His divine grace. A greater blessing never was conferred on mortals. From the birth of Adam until the present day we are taught in our Bible that God wrought miracles upon the Egyptians - brought the children of Israel over the Red Sea - preserved them in the wilderness in safety. But by and by they entered into the land of Canaan, a land of freedom, and immediately they began to have trouble and discord. But you, my colored friends, have been prepared with a perpetual home through life. You are as trees planted by the river of waters, whose branches fail not. O that you might praise the Lord for his goodness and for His wonderful works toward you black people.

Again, God's wisdom is displayed in the institution of slavery, in its great plan of perpetuating the negro race. "The white men, the masterpiece of God's creation." when tracing nature through various windings, while the good Samaritans were seeking upon the face of God's earth for objects of pity and compassion, somehow, very mysteriously, were wafted by the kind breezes of heaven to the burning shores of Africa. There they found the sooty tribes of that hot climate very much degraded. At first they scarcely knew what to call them; they so much resembled the orangoutang as to cause a great controversy among God's people. Finally they were seen to bow with reverence and adore an image of their own making. Again, they were seen warring, slaying and eating each other, and sacrificing one another by thousands to their deities.

This disposition was so much like that of the low class of whites that they felt the spirit of pity and compassion move towards those poor God forsaken creatures, and a plan was immediately formed for their protection and elevation. They were at once taken on board ship, kindly treated, and safely brought to America, where they were put in the care of kind men who provided for them, clothed and fed them, and comforted them in sickness and in health. And here you have been until the present day. Now you can see what God has done for you in instituting this system of slavery. You were found an ignorant set, no top on your heads - and it is doubtful whether you had any soul - more than the apes that played around you. But through the economy of God's grace you have been transplanted upon American soil, and through much toil on the part of the white man, you are becoming quite intelligent. The white man, through amalgamation, has not only imparted to you his straight hair, high nose, blue eyes, thin lips and perfect form, but it is to be hoped that you have a soul much resembling his, which will, by his care and attention, and your obedience to his precepts, stand a great chance to be admitted upon the ground floor of God's glorious temple in heaven - this is better than a thousand lives in Africa, and who would despise his chains, which are but for a moment, and then passeth away - for the blessings which flow out of the system of slavery. The text declares that you shall be slaves your natural lives, which may signify that it is your nature to be slaves. That is, that you are created to be servants of the white man, and all the children to be born of you are to be slaves. Yes, Susan, that little blue-eyed boy you are now trotting upon your knee - the express image of his young master Thomas, is to be a slave, and should you ever see the least disposition of his young master exciting his aspirations to freedom, you must crush that disposition immediately, and repeat to him the language of the text.

Again God's wisdom is displayed in making you with strong constitutions. See what large, robust, fat, greasy looking fellows you all are. See what clear, white teeth you have. Just look at me. See what a puny, slender, delicate, pale looking creature I am, my teeth all decayed. I could not crack parched corn and cotton seeds and get fat like you all do. If I should take a hoe or pitchfork in my hands they would be soiled, and if I should work an hour they would be blistered so badly that I could not correct a slave again for a month. Just look at my hand now. The other day I took hold of a rough cowhide without my gloves on, and gave a young impudent wench, who told my wife something, forty lashes, and it raised this great blister you see. I was never made to work. Look at those great, broad-sided, good, healthy looking wenches sitting before me. What arms they have. Any of them can work from daylight until dark in the field, when the sun is so hot that the overseer has to ride under an umbrella, and your mistress would almost faint just walking out in the garden. Thus, you can plainly see that God has not made the white man to work. He is only to think, plead law, make laws, preach, pray, and carry the gospel to the heathen, and superintend God's works, while the blacks were made to do the hard and dirty work. For this they hard constitutions peculiarly adapted. But again; God's wisdom is further displayed in the economy of slavery by creating you void of natural affections, as regards family sociability, and maternal and parental love for your husbands, wives and children. Therefore, our conscience is void of offense toward God or you negroes, when we separate the husbands from their wives and children, for it is for the purpose of rearing up fine temples for the glory of God and his Kingdom.

ABRAHAM LINCOLN,
Emancipator of over four and a half million slaves; elected President
November, 1860; assassinated April 12, 1865, by Wilkes Booth.

THE LINCOLN LOG CABIN.
The above engraving is from a photograph of the Lincoln cabin; taken especially for this book, Decoration day,
May 30, 1907. The picture shows the cabin just as it stands today on the old Lincoln farm in Hardin Co., Ky.

CHAPTER XVI.

THE SORROW OF PARTING CHILD.

O, tell me papa, when mother dies,
Will she come home again?
Or will we meet above the skies,
Where Christ the Savior reigns?
Would you not like to die tonight,
If mother, too, would die?
And with sweet angels dressed in white,
Meet her above the sky?

FATHER.

O, yes, my child, my life is dear,
And you I love full well;
But I no longer can tarry here,
I soon will bid this world farewell;
I cannot live, my heart is broke,
My grief is more than I can bear;
This very strap and that great oak;
Will end my life in deep despair.

Early Friday morning, April 12, 1861, I took my master to
Wilmington. On the way we stopped and took in another man. As
we neared Wilmington we could hear the booming of cannons, for
the rebels had fired upon Ft. Sumter, and we could hear the echo of
the guns as it came down the Cape Fear river and was borne out on
the broad bosom of the Atlantic. My master, in great excitement,
slapped his hands together, and with an oath, said, "its come." Both
of them grew deathly pale, and looked at each other as though they
were surprised. My master hastily wrote a short note, sealed it and
gave it to me, with directions to hurry home, cautioning me very
particularly not to stop until I reached home and delivered the note
to his wife.

I saw that every white man in Wilmington was greatly agitated and wore a look of anxiety. In a moment everything that had been told me by the Yankee soldiers, and by the underground railroad men, flashed in my mind; for many of them had told me that I would some day be free, and we looked forward to that day with great expectations.

I drove as fast as I could to the five mile farm, which was in charge of the colored overseer. Uncle Tom could read and write, and I wanted to know what was in the note. I had many times slipped him the newspapers from the house, and carried them back early the next morning before master called for them, and he taught me to listen carefully to every conversation held between the white people. I drove up to the fence, where fifty or sixty men and women worked in the field. I could hear them singing and shouting, for they too, had heard the booming of the cannon, and Uncle Tom had told them that that was a token of liberty. But when they saw the old "carry-all" drive up, each one ran to his or her work; the overseer came to the carriage, supposing master wanted to see him, but to his surprise master was not there. He called the slaves around and had me explain how master acted at the sound of the guns, then he made a speech to them, telling them to pray as they had never prayed before. I gave him the note I had for mistress; he looked at the envelope, studied for a moment, rubbed his head, and then thoroughly wet the seal; he opened the letter and read it. The letter read as follows:

"We have fired on Fort Sumter. I may possibly be called away to help whip the Yankees; may be gone three days, but not longer than that. You write a note and send William to Sawyer, [that is the overseer on the farm where we live] and tell him to keep a very close watch on the negroes, and see that there's no private talk among them. Have Martin, the overseer's son, aid you, and if Elliott or Fuller come on the place, give them no opportunity to talk with the negroes.

Your husband,
JOE COWENS."

(This Fuller referred to in the note is the son of the Fuller mentioned in a previous chapter, and who was murdered because he was suspected of being connected with the underground railroad, and also of aiding my father, who had already partially paid for his freedom, trying to get away.)

After reading the note Uncle Tom told me to drive back and go around by the Salisbury road. This took me nearly two miles out of the way, but in the middle of this road was a large mud puddle. He told me to drive in there, very fast, then get out and wade in the water, and get the envelope wet and muddy. He showed me how to smear It over with my hands so mistress would not detect that it had been opened. He also showed me how to make saliva or crocodile tears. He said mistress would be on the porch watching for me, and that I should pretend to cry, at the same time get the envelope from my pocket, handing it to her with the left hand. She would take it with her right hand, tear it open and drop the envelope on the ground. As soon as she was gone I was to pick it up and destroy it. Mr. Fuller was in the house, having come to see master on business, so when mistress heard the carriage coming she came to the big gate to meet it, thinking master was returning, and left Mr. Fuller in the house. When I saw her coming I made some crocodile tears by wetting my fingers with saliva. As soon as she saw that master was not with me, she came rushing to the buggy and found me shedding tears as fast as I could. In a very tender tone, with her hand upon my head, she asked me what was the matter. At this I broke down completely and cried aloud, at the same time feeling in my pocket for the envelope, and telling my sad story, between sobs, of how I had dropped it in the mud hole. She eagerly grasped it and tore it open, not noticing that it had ever been opened before, and patting me on the head, she said, "hush, mistress can read it." That instantly healed my pretended broken heart and dried up my manufactured tears.

She started for the house, forgetting she had not cautioned me, so she came back and told me "that Mr. Fuller was in the house, and for me not to mention anything to him or any one on the place, concerning the cannon firing." She then wrote a note and gave it to me to take to Mr. Sawyer. She had dropped the envelope and I was glad when she was out of sight. Picking up the envelope I put it in my mouth, chewed it up, removed a harness peg, put the pulp in the hole, and replaced the peg. If the old barn is still standing the envelope is there yet. I took the note to Mr. Sawyer and in a short time he was at the house in close consultation with her. Then he went after his son Martin, and they both went over to five mile farm, where Uncle Tom was overseer. She wrote another note to Mr. Bailey, a poor white man living about a mile away, and he came at once and took charge of our farm. He was once overseer on our place , but was so cruel that massa discharged him. So now he served as an extra two or three days at a time for the different overseers in the community, for which he received seventy-five cents per day, and what he could get the slaves to steal for him, for notwithstanding their inhumanity to the slaves, they kept up a constant trade with them. They stole their master's corn, wheat, chickens, hogs, etc., and carried them to the overseer, for which he would give them a little flour, and occasionally a dime or two, and very often when he was about to whip them he would let them off by their promising to bring him some meat or chickens. Master came home that night, and after supper five or six of the leading men from Wilmington came. After I brought in the demijohn, glasses and water, master told me that I could go to bed, because he would want me to go away with him early the next day. But instead of going to bed I pulled off my shoes, tip-toed down stairs and peeped through the keyhole, and not making an exception to the rule, my ear did its share of listening. They got into a hot discussion, and I heard one of them say, "if the Yankees whipped, every negro would be free." I became satisfied that the negro was the bone of contention, and that the light of liberty was probably about to dawn, so I went to bed.

On the morning of April 15th, 1861, I left home with my master to go to the war and whip the Yankees in three days; I carried a club for the first three days to knock off Yankees' horns with, for my master told me that they had horns. We were gone more than three months; we didn't whip them, but were gaining a victory in every battle that was fought, and this was encouraging to the rebels. You could hear the southern ladies singing "Old Lincoln and his hireling troops would never whip the South." We came home on a week's furlough, then returned to be gone six months, but before the expiration of the six months, my master was killed by a shell bursting at Greenville, Tennessee, near the place where John Morgan was killed.

CHAPTER XVII.

At first the northern people were chagrined and disheartened. Then came a renewed determination. They saw the real character of the war, and no longer dreamed that the south could be subdued by a mere display of military force. They were to fight a brave people - Americans - who were to be conquered only by a desperate struggle. During the first year of the war the Confederates had captured the large arsenals at Harper's Ferry, near Norfolk. They had been successful in the two great battles of the year - Bull Run and Wilson's Creek; also in the minor engagements at Big Bethel, Carthage, Lexington, Belmont, and Ball's Bluff. The Federals had saved Fort Pickens and Fort Monroe, and captured the forts at Hatteras Inlet and Port Royal. They had gained the victories of Phillippi, Rich Mountain, Boonville, Carricks' Ford, Cheat Mountain, Carnifex Ferry and Danville. They had saved for the union, Missouri, Maryland, and West Virginia. Principally, however, they had thrown the whole south into a state of siege - the armies on the north and the west by land, and the navy in the east by sea, maintaining a vigilant blockade.

After the death of my master I remained as cook for the company until November, 1863, when at Blue Springs, Tennessee, Generals Thomas and Burnside routed Hood and Forrest, after a short contest; and in the retreat, I, with many others, was captured. I was with the cooks' brigade. There were about fifty of us, and each one was riding one of those long eared fellows, that lean against the fence and say, "I have no one to love me."

In the retreat we had quite a deep ditch, or gully, to cross. My animal was heavily loaded with camp kettles, tin pans and kitchen utensils in general. When the cavalry got to this ditch they commanded their horses to mount, and the horses leaped over, but I suspect in the excitement I forgot to give the necessary commands, for my long eared friend's fore feet reached the other shore safely, but his hind feet fell short of the mark, and down in the ditch we went; such a scramble you never saw. But I found that there were many rebel soldiers in there, who were tired of the Yankee lead and wanted to be captured. I was scrambling to get out, but they told me to lie still, and in a few moments Yankee soldiers - both cavalry and infantry, seemed to have popped up out of the earth; while some pursued the fleeing rebels, others took us to the general's headquarters. The rebels were sent to the northern prisons, and the cooks and colored servants that had been captured, were next brought before General Thomas and disposed of. I was the last man in the line, and when I came before the general, his first words to me were, "you're a fine looking fellow. Here we are fighting to free you and you are here dressed up in a suit of rebel uniform." He then called his cook - a quaint looking, cross-eyed old man, who like myself, was "hewn out of a slab of ebony." He said, "Nathan, what shall we do with this boy?" "Hang him to the highest tree we can find," said Nathan. "Well, bring me the best rope you can find." Nathan obeyed. He came with a rope as large around as his wrist, and about twenty feet long. The general asked him if he thought that would hold me; he answered in the affirmative, and General Thomas told him to throw it over the limb of a tall oak which stood near by. But an officer by the name of Lane rode up and said: "General, maybe this boy will take the oath of allegiance." I would have taken most anything about this time. Then the general inquired of me if I would take the oath. I told him I would. By this time some one said, "hold up your right hand." Another said, "hold up your left hand," another said, "your right foot," and another said, "your left foot." I obeyed orders as fast as they were given until it came to the left foot. I had up all I could possibly get up. After having all the fun they wanted with me, the general told Nathan to take me back and wash and clean me up. Uncle Nathan took me to his tent, where he had a kettle of boiling water. It looked as if he were going to scald a hog; then began the washing process. After the old man had rubbed and washed me until my flesh burned, and I had put on a castaway suit of General Thomas', I went to headquarters. After standing before the large mirror in the general's tent. I thought I was the richest, freest man in America. They had carried the joke to such an extent - for I really thought they were going to hang me - that I was sick. They administered some medicine to me and I lay down across the general's bed, General Thomas himself having told me to. When I awoke about 3 p. m. I was between the two generals, Burnside and Thomas. When I moved towards one he would crowd against me, and if I moved towards the other he would crowd in, until I was squeezed as tightly as possible between the two. They were both awake, and I could feel their sides heaving until they could not restrain their laughter any longer, then General Thomas said, "lie still boy, this white won't rub off." This was my first day of freedom.

General Thomas questioned me concerning my parents, and on learning that my mother was in Greenville, Tennesse, he said; "you will see her within three days if the rebels don't whip us." Accordingly we left Blue Springs that day enroute to Madison Court House, Virginia. which brought us through Greenville where mother was. It was hard to prevent me from being the advance guard. For two days they were trying to hold me back, until we finally reached Greenville, and I saw the house in which mother lived. Seeing that no rebels were near, the officers allowed me to advance. Before I reached the house I saw mother and my Jewish mistress, Mrs. Hadley, standing on the porch. Everybody seemed very much excited, and the rebel army was retreating.

Having changed my uniform from the rebel gray to the Yankee blue, my mother did not recognize me until I was at the gate; then she came running and shouting "this is William." I was saying in one breath - not waiting for one question to be answered before I asked another, "how are you?" I am free, are you? Get ready to go to the Yankees; has master the same black horse and buggy?" She told me he had. I told her to go pack up while I hitched the horse to the buggy. When I returned to the house the soldiers had surrounded it and asked me where my mother was. I ran up stairs. tried to open mother's door, when she informed me that Massa Jake had locked her in. The soldiers were hurrying me to get my mother and come on I told them Massa had locked her in, and one of them gave me an ax and told me to break the door open. I told mother to stand back from the door. At the same time Massa Jake came in with a shot gun in his hand, but before he could raise it dozens of muskets were aimed at him. By this time I had the door open, and there stood mother with a rope around the bureau, and every loose article she could get hold of was wrapped in her straw tick, all tied up ready for moving. She was expecting to move the whole cargo in a buggy.

I had her unpack as quickly as possible and gather up her clothes and little keepsakes, so we could be out of the yard as soon as possible. I shall never forget the courtesy shown mother by two or three soldiers, in helping her in the buggy. Being all ready, and our buggy placed in line with the other contrabands - for there were between one hundred anti fifty and two hundred wagons, mule carts, pack horses, mules and even milch cows, we started on our journey.

Most of the southern men had gone to war, and those who were too old to go had taken the women and gone to the cities, leaving the farms and country homes virtually in charge of the colored people. I had an uncle who was left in charge of a farm three miles from town. We passed by his place on our way to Virginia, and when we came in sight of the farm we could see colored people by the hundreds, who had gathered from other farms. The news spread like wild fire all over the country that the Yankees had come.

The "great house" was kept furnished the year round and left in the colored overseer's charge, because the family would come back and forth, sometimes staying weeks at a time. The veranda was filled with men, women and children, singing, shouting and praising God in the highest. I hastened into the yard and was soon the center of attraction. Uncle Isaac was soon by my side, picking me up and carrying me around, shouting at the top of his voice, while I was struggling to get down, and trying to drown his voice so I could tell him that he was free, and to pack up at once and go with us.

I was inviting him to liberty, yet I had not a shelter in all the world to put my head save the canopy of Heaven. But I had heard of a country where all men were free, and like Bunyan's Pilgrim I had started to make it my home.

I finally succeeded in loosing myself from his strong embrace, and then I made a short speech to all, telling them to hitch their ox and mule carts, and load up their things and go to the Yankees. There was considerable fear about their doing as I said, until some of the soldiers appeared, and helped to dispel this fear by confirming what I had said. It was not long until the yard was fairly lined with wagons, carts and every conceivable beast of burden. They began to tear down their old bedsteads, built against the walls of their cabins, and gather up their rude furniture, when the Yankees asked what was in the "great house." On learning that it was furnished they demanded that it be opened, and that the people take everything they wanted and load their wagons. My uncle had the key but refused to open the door, saying "that belongs to old Master." Fifteen or twenty soldiers then seized a huge log of wood and broke the door down.

'Twas but a few minutes until the great place was gutted. The piano was the only piece of furniture remaining, and some women wanted to take that for their girls when they became educated. Now the wagons were loaded to their utmost capacity. I can't afford to spoil a good joke because of race, color or nationality. Then the children were put on, and it seems to me now that the mothers must have taken some kind of paste and put on the backs of the children, so as to stick them up against the furniture. They were so thick around the wagons it seemed there was not a spot left where there was not a baby. They were of all sizes and colors; they were black, dark brown, pumpkin colored, yellow and half white. And they were all crying with a different voice, giving different tunes to the song they were singing. It was certainly a menagerie when the procession left the farm. Some of the babies were crying alto, some soprano, some bass, but most of them baritone - because it was bare of all music.

Of course all of our masters were honorable, and these children were all called by their master's name - but they didn't call them papa all the time. Many of their mothers were as honorable as a woman could be under the circumstances, but many times in order to save their backs from being lacerated they obeyed the command of their master, and their commands were not always honorable.

The soldiers now moved forward toward Knoxville, Tennessee. We had four or five hundred men, women and children in this great march from a land of servitude to a land of liberty. Sometimes like Pharaoh of old, the old masters would pursue their slaves, and even come into the camp but the slaves' fears would soon be dispelled by the stern command of some Yankee soldier or officer, who would order the rebs to leave the camp. Many times they subjected them to some humiliating treatment - such as riding the rail horse, or carrying a barrel up the hill and rolling it down again, and they would continue this process for hours. After skirmishing for a week or ten days we arrived at Knoxville, Tennessee, where we sold the horses, mules, oxen, buggies and wagons to General Thomas. I bought an old log cabin on the old battle field for my mother. I was to give seventeen dollars for this property. I could count from one to fifty, but I could not tell the denominations; I didn't know a ten dollar bill from a one; so I counted out seventeen bills and paid for the place. Later I learned that I had paid some forty or fifty dollars for it.

About this time, in 1863, Frederick Douglas went to Washington to see President Lincoln, telling him "that our people were digging breast works, exposed to the shot and shell, and why not give them guns and let them have a hand in freeing themselves and saving the union." Lincoln's reply was that the feeling at the north was running so high he didn't know what the result would be, for no measure of the war was more bitterly opposed than the project of arming slaves. It was denounced at the north, and the confederate congress passed a law which threatened with death any white officer captured while in command of negro troops, leaving the men to be dealt with according to the laws of the state in which they were taken. Douglas said he returned home, but slept little that night, for he continually called on God to in some way bring peace out of the confusion, and open the way for colored men to get on the field of battle as enlisted soldiers. The next morning by nine o'clock Douglas said he was at the capitol and closeted with the president. To his surprise Lincoln told him that Grant had sent for a division of colored soldiers. Lincoln commissioned Douglas as recruiting officer, and sent him to Boston Massachusetts, where he mustered in the 54th and 55th colored regiments. These were the first colored regiments organized in the free states.

Col. Shaw led the 54th regiment in its first battle at Fort Wagner. After keeping us in reserve for three hours while the union soldiers were falling like Wheat before the sharpened sickle, Col. Shaw asked to lead the black phalanx into the battle, notwithstanding he knew it meant certain death to him if he was captured, the confederates having said they would not take any union soldier prisoner who was in command of colored troops, for they did not recognize the colored men as citizens or soldiers, therefore would not consider them or their leaders as prisoners of war. Col. Shaw sent his orderly back to the wagon train. He returned in a few moments and handed the Colonel a bundle, which contained a regimental silk flag with the inscription, "To the 54th Colored Regiment, Robert G. Shaw, Colonel. Presented by the White Ladies of Boston, Massachusetts." Our regiment went wild at the sight of the flag. They carried Col. Shaw up and down the line on their shoulders, cheering like mad. As he handed the flag to Carney, the flag bearer, the Colonel said, "Carney, will you return this flag to us in honor?" His answer was, "Colonel, I will do so or report to God the reason I do not." The roll was called and twelve hundred men and officers answered to their names. The battle was on. Our gallant Colonel's side was torn by a shell a few moments after. His dying words were, "boys, don't let the flag go down." His body never touched the ground, being borne to the rear by his colored troops, one of whom was instantly killed. His place was immediately filled by another. Carney's right arm was shot off during the battle. As he fell, holding the flag with his left hand and in his teeth, he shouted, "boys, don't let the flag go down." When the roll was called after the battle seventy-seven had answered to their last roll call, having fallen defending the flag and fighting for their liberty. Colonel Shaw was buried with his many black soldiers who lost their lives in this fierce battle.

At one time, in order to be in season for an assault, these regiments marched two days through heavy sands and drenching storms. After only five minutes rest, we took our place at the front of the attacking column. The men fought with unflinching gallantry, and planted their flags. So willing were the negroes to enlist, and so faithful did they prove themselves in service, that in December, 1863, over fifty thousand had been enrolled, and before the close of the war that number was quadrupled.

I recognized then that I was to take part in one of the greatest wars of modern times. The war of the rebellion was now on, when the numbers engaged in it, and the extent of territory affected are considered. It was primarily a war based on sentiment. The long, but peaceful and prayerful contest of the abolitionist against the slave power, and the earnest and faithful prayer of the slave himself, all crowded the throne of a just God, and had aroused the whole country, so that everywhere, in every state in the union, there was a sharp division of opinion among the people. It is true always, however, that God makes the wrath of man to serve him, and out of the wear of the rebellion the slave fought his way to freedom. What a glorious record the Afro-American made in that war! It is one of the brightest pages in all history. In the early stages of the war he was not even allowed to drive the teams, to dig trenches or to throw up breastworks for the union army. Tile soldiers of the north declared that this was a white man's war, and that sentiment had made it very difficult for the government at Washington to call for colored troops, but before the close of the war he was a regularly enlisted soldier in all the departments, to the number of 200,000, and had fought with such valor, such heroism, from Fort Wagner to Fort Fisher, from New Market Heights to Petersburg, that when the victorious union army at last marched into Richmond, the fallen and deserted capitol of the lost cause, he was accorded the first place of honor at the head of the column! Thirty six years afterwards Colonel Theodore Roosevelt, of the rough riders, commented on the bravery of the black soldiers after the brilliant charge of a successful capture of San Juan Hill. Thirty six years after Colonel Robert Gould Shaw was buried with his negroes, in the sands of Morris Island, the world has looked with enthusiasm upon the heroic deeds and gallantry of the negro soldier, and today he is filling his station from West Point, the military center of the world, to the navy that plows the distant seas and watches the gate way to this nation. This fact is demonstrated when you recall to memory the 25th of January, 1898, when the battleship Maine steamed into the harbor of Havana. She went there on an errand of peace, the representative of a friendly power. On the 15th of February the Maine was blown to atoms by a floating mine, together with two hundred sixty-six American sailors, of whom more than thirty were negroes.

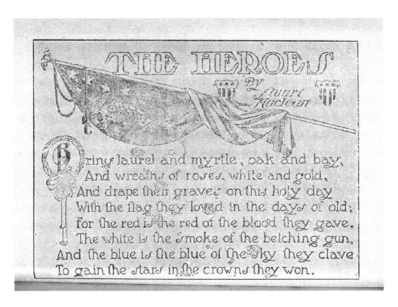

THE HEROES

By Stuart Macleur

Bring laurel and myrtle, oak and bay,
And wreaths of roses, white and gold,
And drape their graves on this holy day
With the flag they loved in the days of old;
For the red is the red of the blood they gave,
The white is the smoke of the belching gun,
And the blue is the blue of the sky they clave
To gain the stars in the crowns they won.

CHAPTER XVIII.

In 1864, near Blue Springs, Tennessee, three union soldiers became separated from their army, and when passing through a small oak grove one of them got into the quicksand. The others, supposing their companion was closely following them, pursued their course.

This poor hero was left behind, struggling for his life in the quicksand, for three days and nights, buoying himself up from sinking, with the aid of such sticks and brush as he could reach. This location was but a short distance from a large southern mansion. The men had all gone to war and there were left but a few old colored mothers to protect the old mistress.

Aunt Nancy Jordan dreamed one night, or saw a vision, as she termed it, that she saw a man in trouble near the springs, and that she heard a voice saying: "Nancy, go to the east spring." She claimed to have heard that call three different times that night in her dreams, and early the next morning she took her pail and went to the spring. When near the place, she heard a human voice pleading for help. She then realized her dream or presentiment, and on looking saw union soldier buried to his armpits in the quicksand. She knew just what it meant, and started toward him. He murmured for her not to come too close. Her reply was "God bless you chile, I knows all about dis place." She felt her way as close to him as possible, or until she felt the quicksand giving way under her, then she gathered brush and bridged her way over to him, or near enough to reach him with a long handled gourd. She then went to the spring, which was not over twenty feet away, and secured water for him, as his tongue was so badly swollen that he could scarcely speak. She held the gourd to his lips, slaked his thirst, and then began the work of rescue, piling brush around him. She then got hold of his arms and assisted him out so that he could sit upon the brush.

That spring was never used by the people from the mansion on account of the quicksand, and alkali in the water. Nancy returned to the house with her pail of water, then hurried back with food in the pail upon her head. In this way she fed him for three weeks, at the end of which time one morning she heard the tramp, tramp of a mighty army. Bands were playing and bugles sounding. Then she saw old Missie scampering for the cellar, for, said she: "Nancy, they are Lincoln's hirelings, for they are all dressed in blue." Aunt Nancy hurried to the spring and told the soldier that the Yankees were coming. He at once came from his hiding place. When he reached the yard of that mansion he found it swarming with union soldiers. He said to Aunt Nancy, "I can't leave you here, for you must go with us." She replied: "I promised old master not to leave old missie till he comes back from de wah." But he assured her that it meant her freedom, and asked if she had not prayed to be free? She replied: "Yas sah," and that if it meant her freedom she would bid old missie good bye.

There was a pathetic scene at this parting. Old mistress ventured to the porch and took her last long look at her old ex-slave, as the Yankee soldier was helping her into the wagon.

Aunt Nancy became cook in the camp for the officers, and this soldier, whom she had rescued, looked after her as though she were his mother. He was an Englishman, and had come to this country about the time of the beginning of the war. He naturalized and enlisted. When he was discharged he took Aunt Nancy to England with him and presented her to his mother as the preserver of his life. She had been in London two years or more when I arrived there, and was among the most honored women of the city.

She came back to America on the same steamer that I came on. She was certainly looked upon as a sanctified christian woman.

The soldier who took her over was bringing her back. He would have her dress in the same costume she wore when she rescued him from the quicksands, and thus gave an exhibition every few days. She was not now the same illiterate Aunt Nancy that she was three years ago for contact with educated and refined people had polished her up wonderfully.

MARTYRED PRESIDENT McKINLEY.

CHAPTER XIX.

THE NEGRO IN IT.

1 In the last civil war,
The white folks they began it.
But before it could close,
The negro had to be in it.

2 At the battle of San Juan hill,
The rough riders they began it;
But before victory could be won
The negro had to be in it.

3 The negro shot the Spaniard from the trees,
And never did regret it,
The rouge riders would have been dead today,
Had the negro not been in it.

4 To Buffalo McKinley went,
To welcome people in it,
The prayer was played, the speeches made,
The negro he was in it.

5 September sixth, in Music Hall,
With thousands, thousands in it,
McKinley fell from the assassin's hand -
And the negro, he got in it.

6 He knocked the murderer to the floor,
He struck his nose, the blood did flow;
He held him fast, all near by saw it,
When for the right the negro is in it.

7 J. R. Parke is his name,
He from the state of Georgia came;

He worked in Buffalo for his bread,
And there he saw McKinley dead.

8 They bought his clothes for souvenirs,
And may they ever tell it -
That when the president was shot,
A brave negro was in it.

9 McKinley now in heaven rests;
Where he will ne'er regret it;
And well he knows, that in all his joys,
There was a negro in it.

10 White man, stop lynching and burning
This black race, trying to thin it -
For if you go to heaven or hell,
You will find some negro in it.

11 You may try to shut the negro out
The courts, they began it,
But when we meet at the judgment bar
God will tell you the negro is in it.

12 Pay them to swear a lie in court,
Both whites and blacks will do it;
Truth will shine, to the end of time,
And you will find a negro in it.

13 If there's a position to be filled,
In congress or in senate,
We people of this nation pray
This negro may get in it.

MRS. LENA MASON.

I enlisted in the 54th Massachusetts, where I remained nine months; was transferred to the 28th Indiana, on account of having an uncle in that regiment. I remained in the army from July, 1863, until

December, 1865. Was in the following regular battles: Battle of the Wilderness, Kenesaw Mountain, Chancellorsville, Virginia, Culpepper, Virginia, Antietam, Maryland, Blue Springs, Missionary Ridge, Nashville, and Greenville, Tennessee and many other skirmishes.

I was mustered out on December 29, 1865, with no home to go to, no starting point or object in life. The rebels had raided Knoxville Tennessee, and mother, with all the colored people, had left there, and I could gain no knowledge concerning her whereabouts. I saw my mother in 1863, when I left her in the little log cabin in Knoxville, and I never saw her again for fifteen years. The medium then used in finding any of our people was the church. Any one looking for a lost relative would send letters of inquiry to all the different churches in the United States and Canada, describing the person, and giving names of masters they had belonged to, so far as they knew. So I tried to find my mother, and at the expiration of a few years I heard of a woman in Huntsville, Alabama, answering the description. There was great difficulty in finding our people because they were sold so often, and had to take the name of each master. Knowing that my mother was a christian woman, and would be identified with some church I wrote to all the churches in Huntsville, and finally received an answer, stating that a woman answering that description had lived there, but not of that name - for I inquired for Rosy Hadley, the name of her last master.

I then went to Huntsville, and after spending a month of constant research and inquiry I had to give it up as futile. I returned to Nashville, but did not give up the search through the medium of letters. Finally I received a letter from Chattanooga. I went there and spent more than two months, but to no avail. After this I heard nothing from her, or concerning her, for over six years. During this time I learned that I had a brother in Philadelphia, Pennsylvania. After the exchange of a few letters we were satisfied that we were brothers, and he came to see me. It proved to be my oldest brother, James, who had run away from Wilmington in 1860. He went to an underground railroad station twelve miles from Wilmington. Here he was put in a box, this box was enclosed in another box, and the second box in a third box, and sent by express to New York, where he was released from his somewhat cramped quarters in Rev. Henry Ward Beecher's parlor. To give him air, holes were bored in each box, care being taken that they were not opposite each other. From New York he went to Toronto, Canada, was educated by the Presbyterian church, serving many years as a pastor. He died in 1890. About three hours before his death he sat propped up in bed, and preached a sermon, using as his text "Blessed is the man who dyeth in the Lord. He shall rest from his labors and his works do follow him." After his remarkable escape he always went by the name of "Box Brown."

Through him I found another brother, who was a locomotive engineer over the Grand Rapids and Indiana railroad. We three were soon together and again began a zealous search for mother, ultimately locating her in Lebanon, Tennessee. It was not long until we found her, though not in Lebanon, for when we reached there we learned that she had been gone from that place nearly a year. She had gone back to Knoxville, in which city I found her, and when she saw me, she exclaimed, like Simeon of old on seeing Jesus, "now Lord let me die in peace, for mine eyes have seen my son William"

That memorable morning, as I left the city of Nashville, with my fireman's uniform on, and two hundred dollars in my pockets, my heart was buoyant with expectation, for it was no more hope, but a grand reality, that I would see the faces of the dearest earthly friends I had - a mother and two sisters. The arrangements for the meeting had been made unbeknown to mother. At train time my sisters were on the alert for me, and as I neared the house they called mother's attention to some one coming. Mother came to the door, walking with a cane; she said, "that walks something like my William." But the sight of mother so elated me that I bent my steps quick and fast toward the house. When I was close enough for her to recognize my face, she uttered the words before stated.

I am lost for language to describe the scene which followed. The only thing which cast a shadow over the pleasure of our meeting was when mother asked, "if we had heard anything from father?" The house of joy was turned into lamentation, but after a while quiet was restored. We never saw or heard from father after he was sold. We learned that another brother, named Andrew, was about eight miles from Knoxville. In a few days he joined us and we spent a glorious time together. There were now mother and six children together - two sisters and four brothers.

CHAPTER XX.

I returned to Nashville - which I considered home - after several weeks' visit with mother. I re-entered on my duties as fireman - for I was a member of the City Fire Department, and had been engaged as hosecart driver for eight months. Shortly after my return we were called out to a large fire. While fighting the fire the captain called to "Jim Howard." After calling several times and no one seemingly hearing him, he called "Jim Cowens," and that attracted my attention. I looked to see who would answer, and seeing a man on top of the house answering, I immediately climbed on the building.

I inquired of Jim "where he came from," and many similar questions, and it was but a few minutes until we recognized each other as brothers. Now you can better imagine what followed than I can express it. It came to the ears of the City Council of the City of Nashville, "that two brothers who had served eight months in No. 2 Hose Company, had just recognized each other as brothers - having been separated for sixteen years." In honor of our meeting they gave us a public reception.

One extreme always follows another, for in three weeks from the time of our recognition, my brother was thrown seventy-two feet from the hook and ladder against the stone custom house, and every bone in his body was broken; he died instantly.

I served seventeen months in the fire department, and resigned to accept a situation as singer and banjo player in a troupe gotten up by S. C. Wallace. The troupe was known as the "Tennessee Singers" (not the original Tennessee Jubilee Singers, yet we attracted the attention of the public at large to the extent that we were constantly in demand.) We made a tour from Nashville, Tennessee, to Indianapolis, Indiana, thence to Terre Haute, Indiana, from there to Chicago, Springfield. Bloomington, Illinois, LaPorte, Indiana, Detroit, Michigan, and Windsor, Canada. On our return trip we sang in the following cities in Michigan: Grand Rapids, Battle Creek, Kalamazoo and Niles, then back through Indiana and Kentucky to

Nashville, Tennessee. We sang nothing but the southern melodies - songs composed by our fathers and mothers in the days of slavery. We disbanded in November, 1868.

In January, 1869, I hired to what was known as the Hanlon's Wizard Oil Company, with seven others, at twelve dollars per month and board. The contract was for one year. If there was any one thing I was accomplished in it was picking the banjo and singing; and I soon became the center of attraction along these lines. We gave street concerts for advertising the oil. We made a tour of the leading cities of Indiana, Illinois and Michigan, thence to New York City, where we took passage, May 21, 1869, on the steamer "City of New York," for London, England.

Everyone treated me so different than I was used to during the time of slavery, that I forgot, to some extent, the hardships through which I had passed, and more than once stopped and inquired of myself "is this heaven, and am I in it?"

The passage over was a very pleasant one, and we arrived in London the 27th day of June, 1869. We neared London - the metropolis of the world. I saw hundreds of vessels, the white winged messengers of commerce , coming from all directions, loaded for London harbor.

The news had been cabled before us that we would arrive June 27th and hundreds of the populace were at the harbor. Their curiosity had been aroused to the highest tension. We repaired to Hotel de France, where we were the center of attraction; hundreds followed the carriages in which we rode to the hotel, and ran over each other in order to get a look at the ladies and gentlemen from America. After supper we went to St. Paul's Cathedral - which had a seating capacity of over two thousand. Here we gave our first concert. The people were wild with enthusiasm, and fairly rained shillings, three cent pieces and bouquets to us on the stage.

At the close of this first concert, a gentleman by the name of William S. Beckenworth, known as Lord Beckenworth, with one son and two daughters, made their way to the stage. After introducing themselves they requested me to go home with them that night, which I could not do without the consent of the manager, Mr. Howard. They at once went to him, and he promised them that I could go the next night, After the sale of medicine the next night I was escorted to the cab by this family, and carried to their home as a guest; and in one single bound I leaped from "Bill Cowens to Lord Cowens, or the Gentleman from America."

Now the great panorama of my life, as a free man, began. My associations were entirely different to those I had been used to - even in my master's home. As I recall that night it becomes a night of wonder to me. As I entered that palace, on St. Mark's avenue, as a guest, they seated me in the center of their spacious parlor, and served me with refreshments. One of the daughters placed a napkin across my chest and gave me a server, upon which were several varieties of very fine fruit. Eighteen or twenty of their friends were present, and all except myself seemed to enjoy the luxuries to the highest extent. This being my first time to be served on social equality with white people, of course I was very much embarrased. I put some of the most delicate fruit in my mouth, but it seemed almost impossible for me to masticate it, for the longer I chewed it the larger it seemed to grow, until I could not swallow. Of course I told them that I was not hungry and did not care for the refreshments, but way down in my heart I was wishing that I had the server, with the refreshments upon it, behind the house - in a few minutes they would have known that I had been there. After a time, pitying my embarrasment, the tray was removed, and I was asked to tell them something of myself and family.

I entertained them for an hour and a half or two hours, and the party retired for the night: but before leaving each one gave me a shilling, and left with the understanding that I was to tell them more about my people the next night. After the father had family prayer they showed me the room I was to occupy and bade me good-night.

After locking the door, and carefully examining the windows with a scrutinizing eye, I searched every crack and crevice in the room, Then I got under the bed and felt the springs. I had heard my master, years before, tell about trap doors under the beds in New Orleans, and that people would get into bed only to find themselves in some dark alley. They had passed through a trap floor and down a slide. Of course, in these cases, the motive was robbery. I don't know why I was fearful, since I had no money save what the people had given me. But the great, unsolvable mystery surrounding me was, why I, an ex-slave, should be paid such high respect among strangers.

There was a night shirt for me to sleep in, also a breakfast gown of heavy velvet. I examined both these articles of comfort laid them back where I found them, took both the sheets off the bed and folded them up, laid them on a chair and climbed in bed. I began to sink so fast in the middle of the big feather bed - had anyone been on the outside they could have heard me gasping and catching my breath - for with all my careful searching for the trap door I thought I was gone, but I finally landed on my pillow of repose.

The second night was almost a repetition of the first. I was like the country lad who went to the city to visit a lady friend. He used a little of the weed. Not being accustomed to use a cuspidor he spat over in a corner. The lady noticing it, pushed the cuspidor to one side of him. He shoved it away. She tried putting it in front of him. Finally, in desperation, he blurted out, "if you don't take that gol darned thing away I'll spit in it." I looked at the night shirt and said to myself, "if that is here another night, I will put it on," also the breakfast robe, I thought the same thing concerning it. So the third night, finding the night shirt still there, I put it on; the next morning on going down to breakfast I put on the breakfast robe. I saw the girls cast glances at each other and wink, as much as to say "he's learning."

I was in England eleven months and a half, and during that time I slept only three nights out of Lord Beckenworth's house. We went to the different hamlets, as far as forty miles from London, but always returned there at night. The roads in London were so carefully kept that you could drive forty miles there while driving half that distance in America. But the first five months of our time were spent principally in the different cathedrals and opera houses in London.

During the first three or four weeks of that time there were from twenty to twenty-five guests at Lord Beckenworth's house every night to hear me talk about my slave life. But after that his two daughters conceived, and put into execution, the grandest thought that could have entered their minds. That was, to try to instill in me the idea of education. They bought books and started on their laborious work, excusing the visitors that came each night, and inviting them to come only on Friday nights, and this they did in large numbers. At first the two sisters were both teachers, one sitting in class with me while the other taught, and vice versa. Many nights we sat up from 10 to 12 o'clock - for I was very anxious to learn. After getting rudiments in my mind I learned with surprising quickness, and knew my letters as if by magic. I could have worn out both of these girls physically, so they decided to take turn about, one each night. And for ten consecutive months I attended school in this home, these two angels of mercy being my teachers. They were faithful, tireless and unfeigned in their efforts to give me some educational light. When I got so I could spell words of two syllables I was like the old fellow when he had learned his alphabet. He said "he had too much edification to stay here or any whar else."

Once a week the visitors would attend in large numbers to see how much I had advanced, and I delighted very much in reciting before them. They were very much amused when I came to spell certain words, especially "baker." I spelled it in that dialectical way, pronouncing each syllable in such a way that it would cause a burst of laughter each time. As I have said before, I learned very rapidly, had an uncommon verbal memory, and in eight months' time was able to read plain reading and could write fairly well. I recall the first letter I wrote. It was to Ulysses S. Grant, at that time president of the United States. I wanted to write to the greatest man in the world, and I thought after Lincoln Grant was next. I reminded him of an incident that occurred during the battle of Kenesaw Mountain, in 1864. He and his staff rode up, a tree limb knocked his hat off, and I thoughtlessly stepped out of my ranks, picked up the hat and handed it to the general. I received a very severe reprimand from my captain, but General Grant called him and in a few words, unheard by me, he satisfied the captain. Then he said to me, "boy, if we both live to get out of the war, let me know where you are and I'll remember you for this favor."

So I wrote to President Grant, informing him that I was alive, and had risen from the ranks of a private soldier in the union army to a Lord, (in title but not in wealth) in England. Miss Emeline - the older daughter of Lord Beckenworth, wrote also, as I dictated and wrote - for I spoke audibly every word I wrote. Of course, when I had finished my letter it looked as if blueing had been poured into a plate and a chicken had walked into it, then over the paper. All the lawyers in the United States could not have read it. But Miss Emeline's letter was enclosed with mine. This was the first letter I ever wrote in my life, and a day or two after I mailed it I began to trouble the postmaster. I went twice a day, expecting an answer from my letter, not considering it had to cross the sea. I was like two negro men, one a runaway from the south, who had crossed the line and gotten safely into the north; the other was a barrister in the north. The runaway negro inquired of the lawyer the way into Canada. The latter scratched his cranium for a moment, cleared his throat, pulled off his gloves, looked over his spectacles and said, "well, sa-ar, if you go by de steamboat and it blowed down whar is you? If you go on the steam kears and dey blowed up, dar you is; but if you go on the junegraph (meaning telegraph) you are dar now."

I wrote my letter to America and thought by the day it was "dar now." But in about thirty days the post master was made glad, and I made to rejoice. It certainly must have been a source of joy to him to be honored with the privilege of handing me the first letter I ever received for myself in my life; but he must have been gladdened to be relieved of a troublesome customer. The president paid me a very high compliment for the exalted station I had reached in so short a time, and invited me to visit the White House on my return to America. He advised me to remain in England until I was thoroughly polished at the hands of this noble family, so that I might return a useful man to my race and the nation. He wrote Miss Emeline a fine letter, commending me as a soldier, and thanking her for the interest she and her sister had taken in the new citizen of America, hewn out of a slab of ebony.

Eleven months spent almost entirely away from my people, save a few hours at night, and constant association with the Caucasian race, wrought quite a wonderful change in myself and habits. As association breeds assimilation, I had gotten almost entirely rid of that southern dialect. My aspirations began to mount above my environments and from that time I began to seek higher things in life. The spirit of manhood which lay slumbering in my breast began to awaken.

This ambition to make something of myself was further strengthened by an incident which occured at this time. Frederick Douglas, marshall of the District of Columbia, was paying London a visit. Queen Victoria, in order to give the people an opportunity of seeing this great man, took him in the royal carriage through the principal streets of the city. The carriage was drawn by twelve horses, and each horse was led by a man in uniform. All London turned out to do honor to America's famous colored orator. The sight of Mr. Douglas as he stood up in the carriage, hat in hand, his silvery hair falling to his shoulders, bowing right and left to the crowds of people who were shouting themselves hoarse in their enthusiasm, fired me with the desire to become a public speaker.

Soon I began to get ready to embark for America again. I had made many friends during my stay in England, who proved to be friends indeed, for the night before my departure they gave me a grand reception, two hundred and twenty dollars and enough clothing to last me a year. This was to enable me to attend school, and every year for four years, they sent me fifty dollars. It was as sad to me parting from these English friends as it ever was to part with my brothers and sisters. When I got in the carriage the next day dozens of friends stood around bidding me adieu, and God's blessings. But thank God, I am not returning the same "William Cowens," in appearance or knowledge, as when I left; for new thoughts and new ideas, that had lain slumbering under the iron heel of oppression for twenty-one years, groaning for light and liberty, are now awakened, and thank God, the light of a new day is dawning upon me.

On board the vessel, instead of entertaining the guests with banjo picking and southern songs, I could talk of things of a higher life, and the passengers soon became interested in me. So much so that for thirty nine days a gentleman, by the name of Joseph P. Ray, and his wife, became my tutors; taking up my lessons where I had left off in England, hearing my last lesson the day we landed in New York.

STEPHEN D. LEE.
Commander-in-Chief Confederate Veterans.

I wandered around this large city for two months trying to find a permanent location, but everything seemed either to high or too fast for me, so I decided to go back to Nashville, Tennessee. I soon put my decision into execution and arrived in Nashville in June. The Methodist Episcopal established a school known as the Freedman's Bureau, from which sprang the great Central Tennessee College. At this time it was only an obscure log hut; today, it is the Atheneum of Education. I entered school here, and continued three years, until my money was exhausted. I then went to work half the day and attended school the other half, and continued in school in this manner for one term. Many times I had nothing in my dinner pail but corn bread and stewed apples. Often I was ashamed for others to see how I was faring, and went off by myself to eat my lunch. My teacher, noticing that I had about the same thing each day, asked me if I never ate anything else but corn bread and dried apples. I felt very much humiliated to tell her that that was all I was able to have. She encouraged me very much by telling me of others that had become great men in this country, who had had even less opportunities than I, yet they pushed their way to the topmost round of the ladder of fame. She also told me that a path of great success was before me, if I only continued as I had started. After that day she never failed to divide her dinner with me. I learned very fast under her, but finally had to quit school entirely and go to work. I worked one year - taking care of three different persons' horses, and making fires in the winter. I saved my money, and when school opened the next year I started again. After that term I went to night school.

CHAPTER XXI.

In 1874 I entered the freshman class in college: I met with another embarrasment here, for every one in the class was ahead of me. As I did not complete the high school course it made it more difficult for me in college. But I had that spirit of determination, and studied with a will, and by the close of the term I had caught up with all the class but three; had made many friends, and was considered by all far from being the dullest boy in the class.

About this time I became very much interested in politics, and the issue of the day was so common that it did not require a man of great ability to become a stump speaker. All I had to do was to remind my people of the fact that the Yankees freed them, and that these Yankees were the present republican party; frequent mentioning of the name of Abraham Lincoln would stir all the patriotism there was in them. I soon became very popular among my race, so much so that I was consulted on every point of the least importance. I was an ardent lover of books, and read quite extensively. I would read many nights all night, and my memory served me well. It was the height of my ambition to be a political orator, for I had in me that retaliating spirit, and thought there was no better way to give vent to my feelings towards the southern people than to tongue-lash them in politics. But after consulting a few men I saw that I had the wrong spirit, and that if I accomplished anything it must be through the spirit of love and not of vengeance. If I wanted to be a useful man to my people and country, I would have to learn "that vengeance belongeth to the Lord."

Later I was hired at Lebanon, Tennessee, as teacher. I had a class of forty. The majority of them was old people forty-five and fifty years old. I taught them two terms - each term being only four months. The other four months in the year I worked at most anything I could catch. I became impatient with that slow way of making money, so I resigned my school and went back to Nashville. Through a friend I was given a situation as porter for the Woodruff Sleeping Car Company, which was afterwards bought out by the Pullman

Company. I continued in the employment of George L. Pullman for six consecutive years, during which time I was on every road of any importance in the United States and old and New Mexico.

While running from Mackinaw City, Michigan, to Cincinnati, I came near being killed. At Ft. Wayne, Indiana, I stepped off my car while in motion, and was dragged seventy-two feet on my back, all the while hanging to the boxing of the car, the wheels running between my legs. The people turned their backs to keep from seeing me cut to pieces. As the car stopped I relaxed my hold, and they picked me up unconscious, and for some time they thought that life was extinct. They telegraphed my wife that I was dead, but finally I regained consciousness and was returned home that night on the same train. This laid me up for three months.

After I was restored to my natural strength I accepted a position on board a steamboat on Lake Michigan, as steward or cook, for the Graham Passenger Steamboat Company, plying between St. Joseph and Benton Harbor, Michigan, and Chicago, Illinois. During this time I saw some very stormy seasons. I especially recall one of them - the night the Alpena went down with her human cargo of seventy souls. I was on the steamer Traitor, enroute for Chicago from Green Bay; it was one of the most ferocious seas - so said some of the old captains who had sailed the sea for many years, that they had ever seen. We answered the signals for help sent out by the ill-fated Alpena. Our captain called a council to decide whether we would attempt to go to her aid in the midst of the terrific storm then raging. It was unanimously agreed to take our chances, and the ship was turned about, several times nearly capsizing. Before we succeeded in reaching her the signals ceased and we knew that our efforts had been in vain, for the beautiful steamer Alpena, with every soul on board, had gone down to a watery grave. We finally weathered the storm and landed safely in Chicago harbor. On the return trip I fell over board and had a very narrow escape from death, but the captain soon hauled his vessel to, and picked me up after I had gone down and come up the second time.

In 1877, while cooking at the New England hotel, in Clark street, Chicago, I was one night in the third story of a gambling den, owned and run by two brothers - Dan and Jim Scott, two very wealthy colored men. They kept hotel, roomers, and ran a gambling den, all in one building. I had drifted away during my railroad and sailing careers into a class of company that led me to this miserable life. It seemed for a time that all the good that had been accomplished through my many friends, and self denial and perseverance, were all overshadowed with darkness, in immorality and sin. But thank God, on New Year's night, 1877, while standing at the gambling table, I heard my mother's voice, as I thought, as audibly as I ever heard it in my life. She said, "my son," in that tender, motherly way in which none save a mother can speak, "is this what you promised me when you were wearing the shackles of bondage?"

I at once recalled the day when mother left me in Wilmington to go back to Greenville, Tennessee, when she said, "son, I have nothing in this world to give you, but remember that manners and good behavior will carry you through the world; get the religion of Jesus in your heart, and if we never meet again on earth meet me in heaven." I resolved on that night that I would not stop until I was converted. All the entreaties and prayers of my mother came rushing upon my mind, and I decided at once that they should not be in vain. My mind fully made up, I left the gambling den that night, never to enter it again.

The next day I accepted a situation as head cook in Evanston, Illinois, eighteen miles from Chicago. I was deeply convicted and began to reason of righteousness, temperance and the judgment to come. The more I reasoned, the deeper was my conviction, until it seemed that the clock on the wall as it ticked said "repent." I became so interested concerning my soul's welfare, that I could not keep my mind on my business, so I began to seek the Lord in prayer. In June of the same year I walked out of the hotel about eleven o'clock, didn't stop to draw my money; the train was due for Chicago and was at the depot when I arrived there. I was so completely absorbed in thought, and stirred about the salvation of my soul that I walked by the train, up the track towards Chicago. It seemed as though a voice was constantly saying to me, "repent." I had not walked very far when a voice said, "you had better pray." Of course it was the reasoning of the spirit within. I walked down the embankment and for the first time since I was ten years old, I called on God for redemption through the blood of Jesus. I became so intensely earnest that I did not notice the section hands working near by. I arrived in Chicago about dusk, went to a saloon and called for a drink - a very unusual thing for me, because I never went into a saloon before alone. I had often taken a drink through the influence of company. But now, Satan, finding that I was trying to extricate myself from sin, and from the wrath of a sin avenging God, made his greatest struggle to impede my progress. He knew that the wine cup was a sure remedy to carry out his wishes. I never was a lover of strong drink, but now I walked up to the bar and called for gin, as one of the regular hard drinkers would do.

This was one of the remedies that the devil furnished me to drive away trouble, but it failed in this case; for I took two drinks and it took no effect whatever upon me, for my soul was crying for deliverance. I left the bar room, went to the Union depot and bought a ticket for La Porte, Indiana, but I got off at a little station before I got to La Porte, as I thought of a Baptist preacher I knew about three miles from there. It was midnight, and very dark when I got off the train. I inquired of the depot agent the way to this preacher's home. The road lay through a dense, thick woods, and after wandering until about two o'clock in the morning I found the place.

I remained at his home about three weeks, and would go each day to the woods with him and help him pile up brush, trim trees, etc. I imagined all the while that a tree was going to fall upon me and kill me. The very axe the preacher was chopping with seemed to be crying "repent," and I became so troubled that all hunger and thirst seemed to have left me. There was but one thought uppermost in my mind and that was, "that I might find peace with God."

One day the preacher persuaded me to stay at the house, saying I was too weak to go with him to the woods. He knew what was ailing me, I could tell that in his morning and evening devotion, as he would offer me to the throne of grace with so much fervor. After he was gone I took the shot gun, saying to his wife that I would go hunting. I had gone but a short distance when something seemed to say to me, "you might as well take that gun and blow your brains out." Of course this was the reasoning of the devil, making his last great effort to decoy me and destroy my soul. But God has promised in His word that He will be a help in every time of need, and this great truth demonstrated itself to me in this hour of peril, for when my foot had almost slipped, and my soul was almost into eternity - where hope is a stranger, and mercy could never reach my undone condition, the great spirit of God whispered in my soul, "woe be unto your damnation."

I hid the gun beneath a brush pile, and started to a man's house about two miles away. As soon as I went into the house he told his wife to hurry dinner and clean up the dinner dishes, and that they would have a word of prayer. I knelt down behind a big drum stove in that log cabin, with my mind fully made up to stay there until God converted me; and in less time than it will take me to tell it I was happily converted to Christ.

CHAPTER XXII.

It seemed as though I had been wearing a heavy logging chain about my body, and in a moment it fell from me. It looked as if the entire end of the house had given way, and I could see with that eye of faith into the very kingdom of God. I expect one day to behold Christ in His glory, yet I am satisfied that I shall never see Him any plainer, and He will never look any more natural than He did that day in my vision. While beholding this great panorama, Christ handed me a little testament, and pointed towards a large body of woods, saying, "preach my word to these people." In a moment every tree was transformed into a vast multitude of people, and I stepped upon a stump, and began to preach from Romans, First Chapter and sixteenth verse - "Now I'm not ashamed of the gospel of Christ; for it is the power of God unto salvation to every one that believeth; to the Jews first, and also to the Greek."

I need not say to any soul that has been awakened by the light of the gospel that we bad a wonderful downpouring of the spirit that day, and of all the places on earth, that is the dearest to me.

I had worn the shackles of a literal bondage for fifteen years, but in due season God emancipated me from being the goods and chattels of other men, so I could think and act for myself as a man; but thank God, in 1877, he liberated my soul from a greater bondage, for human bondage enslaves only the body, while sin enslaves both soul and body. But I can now praise God in the highest and sing this song, composed and sung by my people of the southland. It was a song of notification, and alluded to the underground railroad and their preparation for escape into Canada.

"Free at last, free at last,
Thank God Almighty, I'm free at last.

1 When I was a sinner just like you,
Thank God Almighty, I'm free at last,

I prayed and mourned till I came through,
Thank God Almighty, I'm free at last.

2 I never shall forget that day,
Thank God Almighty, I'm free at last;
When Jesus washed my sins away,
Thank God Almighty, I'm free at last.

3 The very time I thought I was lost,
Thank God Almighty, I'm free at last;
My dungeon shook and my chains fell off.
Thank God I'm free at last.

4 This is religion, I do know,
Thank God Almighty, I'm free at last;
For I never felt such a love before,
Thank God Almighty, I'm free at last."

The first night after I was converted, I lay down before the fire place - for it was a log house, with a large, old fashioned fire place. The preacher and his family were eating supper in the same room. He said he had not stopped talking to me over five minutes when he noticed me clapping my hands and praising God. But in that few minutes I had found myself in a dense wilderness; I could hear the howling and roaring of some kind of a hideous beast that would strike terror to any living soul, and all was gloom and darkness around me. By faith I looked towards the hill of Zion, and, like Peter of old, I cried out, "Lord, save me or I perish." In a moment the darkness dispersed, and the light, in all its splendor and beauty, shone around me. The same man who handed me a testament in the first vision, gave me the same kind of a book, pointed to the trees and said, "preach My word to these people." In a moment every tree and hush was transformed into a multitude of people. I stepped upon the stump and preached from the same text as before. This was Saturday night and I was sixteen miles from La Porte, Indiana.

Sunday morning the preacher, Rev. Bailey, and myself started for La Porte. There were no trains on Sunday morning, so we rode half the distance on a hand-car with the section men, and walked the remainder of the way. We sat on a fence to rest, facing a beech woods, and I rested my head in my hands and closed my eyes. I had a repetition of the same vision, this being the third time that I saw the same thing. I did not tell this part of my conversion for two years afterwards, for I was satisfied that it was a Divine call to the ministry of the Lord Jesus. Ultimately, an old minister, by the name of Andy Ferguson, a member of the A. M. E. church, who was traveling the La Porte circuit, - after hearing me talk in class meeting several times, asked me to tell him exactly how I was converted. After two years I told him the whole story of my conversion, and he said, "son, I knew God had called you to the ministry." I was wonderfully moved to preach the gospel but felt that I could not afford to give up my occupation of cooking, at which I was making from seventy-five to a hundred dollars per month. for an uncertainty. I knew how hard it was to raise money for the ministers, and like Jonah, I went for nearly five years before I entered the field of labor which God would have me do.

I made several vows and broke them. Finally I vowed if I could accumulate a certain amount of money I would take up the cross and bear it the best I could. I made and saved the amount so quickly that I hardly knew how it came, and avenues were opened to my advantage on every side.

I joined the Missionary Baptist church, though I was of Methodist belief; hut I was cooking where there was no other church save the Baptist. I joined them and gave them fifty dollars toward the building of a new church, with the understanding that if ever a Methodist church was organized there they were to give me a letter of recommendation, and refund twenty-five dollars to the Methodist church. I was soon made a member of the Chain Lake Association of Michigan.

In 1884 a Methodist church was organized and although I was not there, the Baptists refunded the twenty-five dollars. I remained in the Baptist church until 1891, when I joined Simpson's Chapel M. E. church, Indianapolis, Indiana. I was admitted that same year as a member of the Indiana District conference. In March, 92, at Shelbyville, Kentucky, Bishop Foster took up my credentials as elder in the Baptist church, and gave me a sheep skin or credentials, as elder in the Methodist Episcopal church.

CHAPTER XXIII.

In 1877 I married Miss Alice Goins, of Riverside, Michigan, who held up my arms in the ministry for sixteen years while I tried to preach Christ. There were born to us three children, Dora, Marguerite and William. William died in his infancy. The grim monster, consumption, seized upon my companion, and for five years she bore up like a heroine, many times almost compelling me to go to church and preach, when I was fearful that she would die before I returned. But she would say, "my dear, I'm all right, you may save one soul tonight." She would also quote that passage of scripture: Luke 15th Chapter and 10th verse, which reads, "Likewise I say unto you, there is joy in the presence of the angels of God over one sinner that repenteth."

On the morning of April 14, 1892, she sat in the door of our home in Grape Creek, Indiana, looking so constantly and distant that it attracted my attention. I asked her what she was looking at so steadily, and her answer was like a thunder bolt to my heart. She said, "I am looking at the beautiful carpet this day for the last time on earth, for I shall eat my supper in heaven tonight." She had me call our daughters. When they came she said, "girls, I am going to leave you and papa. I want you to hold up your papa's arms as I have done for the last sixteen years. I want you to stay with him until he marries again." She then said to me, "William, I want you to marry as soon as you can find some settled woman. I know you could easily marry some young girl, for you don't look very old, but I want you to marry a settled woman." She continued by saying, "William, you know how I used to set the light in the window for you, and watch for you to come home when I was not able to go with you to your preaching place." I said, "yes, Alice." "Well," said she, "I will set the lamp in the window of heaven, and will wait and watch for you until you come." "Dora, I don't want you to do anything that will hinder your father in the ministry, and pray for him daily that God may sustain him in his labor; be a good girl and meet mamma in heaven."

I called in my family physician; he was so wonderfully touched with the spiritual force and power with which she talked that he could scarcely contain himself. He wrote upon the back of a book, saying: "Reverend, your wife can live but a very short time," and bade me good bye.

The incident relative to the lamp occurred in Lexington, Kentucky, while I was holding a series of revival meetings. She was so low that we did not like to leave her alone while we were at church, but she insisted on the lamp being placed on a table near the bed, so she could read, and said that just at 9:30 she would put it in the window. We could see the light when we reached the top of a hill, and she said, "if you do not see the light in the window when you get to the top of the hill you will know that I have passed over the river." I recall different times when I thought I had reached the spot where I should see it, and not seeing it fell in despair, thinking she had gone, but others ran ahead and told me that the light was in the window.

None but they who have passed through the trying ordeal of the loss of a wife or husband can sympathize with one in this dark and trying hour.

At half past eight that night members and friends filled my home; at eight forty-five she began to sing a song which she used to sing while in health, "I know my name is written in the Lamb's book of life, I know my name is written in heaven." A few minutes before nine she took my hand and said, "husband, have I been a good wife?" With the very fountains of my heart running over with grief I could say nothing else but "yes, a thousand times, yes."

Though it was my daily study to make her happy yet I could never be able to pay the debt of gratitude I owe her. I feel that all that I am I owe to her for her patience and kindness towards me; for when I would despair, and the gloom of disappointment would gather around me, she would put her arms around my neck, kiss me, and say, "papa, let's pray," and in that plaintive, simple way she would take me and my troubles to God. It was her constant study to see and know that I was happy.

Five minutes past nine the chariot swung low, and a loving wife and mother was gone, as we thought. I was on my knees by the bed, with her head resting on my arm; in my excitement I raised her up, and she opened her eyes, sang another verse of the same song, asked the church to take care of her husband and daughters, bade us all good bye, and in a moment her spirit had moved out of the old tenement house of clay, and she

> "Is now drinking at the fountain,
> Where she always will abide;
> For she has tasted life's pure water
> And her soul is satisfied."

I can never describe that night of sorrow, but thank God the consolation which she left in her dying testimony, and her life for sixteen years, sustained me through every conflict, and has been a great source of joy since her departure. Often since that night, when the clouds would hang low and heavy over me, in my imagination I could hear her say, "be of good cheer."

CHAPTER XXIV.

After the funeral services of my wife I returned to my lonely home and tried to make some plans for the future. Left with two girls one a small child, I was forced to take almost a new start in life. Keeping the younger girl, Marguerite, in school, my daughter Dora and I went out to battle with life and for the Kingdom of God. Many trying incidents and perplexities came to me but the tender, loving voice that had encouraged me in days gone by was hushed in death, and I must needs meet them almost alone.

Finally my plans were laid for five years of Evangelistic service. We began our work in Michigan, and the result of our first year's labor was over eighteen hundred souls brought to Christ. The next year I purchased a tabernacle, with a seating capacity of over fifteen hundred. I hired four good singers, and that was indeed a wonderful year. My record showed over two thousand saved. We then went to Indiana, and for three consecutive years continued in this line of work, after which I accepted the pastorate of a circuit at Greenfield and Martinsville Indiana. We built a splendid church at Martinsville. From here we went to Laurenceville, Illinois where our success was wonderful.

In this town a saloon keeper was happily converted one night. He invited the congregation and myself to his saloon at nine o'clock the next morning for a feast. Curiosity brought a large crowd at the appointed hour. When we had gathered, the saloon keeper, with two other men, rolled out three barrels of whiskey, several kegs and cases of beer and other intoxicants, and broke them open. Whiskey and beer ran like water in the streets, and the town was intoxicated with the fumes. We praised the Lord for this external instead of internal application.

After two years in this town I returned to Evangelistic work, and have continued in it until the present time. Great meetings have been held in Ohio, Illinois and Wisconsin. The greatest meeting in Illinois was about three years ago. In eight weeks we saw nine hundred people converted and added to the different churches. In Waymond Chapel, Chicago, we held an all night meeting, at which there were seventy conversions. The church quickened and spiritualized, for which I give God the glory.

My daughter Dora helped me in my work until 1897, when she married and went to live in San Francisco, California. Three years later she was taken suddenly ill. After a partial recovery her husband was bringing her to Louisville, Kentucky, to spend the summer with us. Upon reaching Chicago she was taken worse and was hurried to a hospital. I received a letter one morning, asking me to meet her in Chicago. The same afternoon a telegram came from her husband, telling me to come at once if I would see her alive. I started on the first train. I shall never forget that race with death. I reached Chicago the next morning, but too late; her spirit had taken its flight. Her dying words were, that she had gone to join mother, and for me to meet her in glory. With God's help I expect to do so.

CHAPTER XXV.

THE CHILD'S INQUIRY.

As much as unfeeling men talk and preach about "Negro insensibility," and as much as slavery dotes upon her mysterious power of blotting out and annihilating the principles of humanity, yet it is plainly seen that God has planted in the bosom of the black man a quality of His own nature, that the ruthless hand of time and the strong arm of oppression has not extinguished.

To make my point clearer I will explain the usual form of marriage between house slaves. When a couple wished to marry, if the marriage was agreeable to the owners, a wedding feast was spread by them, the colored people furnishing coon, possum and sweet potatoes. When everything was ready the old negro preacher, (who by the way could not read a word) went through a certain form prescribed by the master. If the couple marrying was young, the young mistresses held a broom stick knee high. If the bride and groom were more advanced in years, older ladies held it. At the end of the ceremony the colored preacher said to the bride and groom, "now, when you jump the broom stick I announce you man and wife." This is how the expression you are all so familiar with originated.

I will relate an incident which came under my observation, which will better illustrate this marriage farce. A loving couple, united in the usual way, had lived in harmony for five years and eight months, during which time not a cloud of discord had come between them; nothing had marred their peace but the thought that they must spend their lives in the midst of groaning and cracking of whips, of which they themselves must share a common fate. To make the nuptial ties stronger they had been blessed, as they thought, with a little girl, whose dark eyes and waving hair satisfied Henry that the child was his. One pleasant evening a South Carolinian was seen talking with the master of that happy pair, and coming before the door they both came to a full halt, while the stranger gazed full in the faces of the three, and after a few moments, passed in profound silence, he said to the master: "I'll give it." As they turned away from the door, the silence was broken by a low whisper from the lips of little Mary, saying, "one of us is sold, papa." Like the disciples, they each asked, "is it I?" Morning found them undisturbed, and Mary hurried the work over, and as usual, left the cabin for the cotton field, repeating in her mind, "is it I?" So excited was her mind that she spent another sleepless night, and so conscious was she that she was the victim [from reading in the eye of the Carolinian his predominating passions], that when she left the house she kissed her child and pressed it against her bosom as though she would crush it to death. Reluctantly she closed the door and departed, to return no more forever. The husband's ears were made sad at noon, when a slave boy said to him, as he called him to the gate, "your wife is sold to South Carolina! I saw her chained in the gang and the last words I heard her say, were, "0! that I had never seen a husband! O! that I had hugged my child to death this morning." But the child's inquiry and the father's answer will show whether humanity was extinct in them:

THE INFANT'S DREAM.

CHILD.

"O, where has mother gone, papa?
What makes you look so sad?
Why sit you here alone, papa?
Has anyone made you mad?
O, tell me, dear papa.
Has master punished you again?
Shall I go bring the salt, papa,
To rub your back and cure the pain?

FATHER.

Go away my child, you are too bad;
You notice things too soon;
Did you not see that I was sad,

From Log Cabin to the Pulpit; or, Fifteen Years in Slavery

When I came home at noon?
Go to the gate and call mamma,
And see if she's in sight.
The hour is late, I fear your ma
Will not be home tonight.

CHILD.

O no, papa, I am afraid
To go to the gate alone;
I fear there's men in the high grass laid,
To catch little Mary Jones.

But what makes mother stay so long?
'Tis getting very late.
Papa, go bring my mother home,
And I'll stay at the gate.
When mother left me early this morn,
She kissed me and she wept;
I saw the tears come trickling down
Upon the pillow where I slept.
She pressed me to her bosom, hard,
As though it was the last embrace.
She sobbed, but did not say a word,
Nor would she let me see her face.

FATHER.

Pull off your shoes, my dearest child,
And say your evening prayer;
And go to bed and after a while,
Perhaps your mother will be there.
Go hush those little eyes to sleep,
And dream some pretty dream tonight,
Perhaps in the morning when you wake
You'll find all things all right.

CHILD.

O' tell me, papa, don't drive me away,
'Tis dark, the stars are thick and bright.
Is mother sold. O, tell me, I pray,
I fear she'll not be home tonight;
O come papa, come go with me,
Perhaps we'll meet her in the lane;
And then she'll sing a song to me,
And take me in her arms again.

FATHER.

Come here my daughter, come to me,
I find that I must tell you true,
Come now, and sit upon my knee -
The dismal tale I'll tell to you.
Your mother's sold; she's sold, my dear,
Her face you'll see no more.
Her cheering voice no more you'll hear
On this side of Canaan's peaceful shore."

CHAPTER XXVI.

I have gone by the name of "Cowens" in this history, and the reader may be curious to know how I came by the name of "Robinson" as I have not mentioned any of my masters by that name.

Two of my masters were named Cowens, one was Robert E. Lee commander-in-chief of the confederate army, another was Scott, and the fifth was Hadley.

I have told you that my father was prince of a tribe in South Africa known as the Madagascar tribe. They heard the ficticious story of Robinson Cruso. In the African dialect the definition was "Rob-o-bus-sho," meaning Robinson Cruso.

An aunt, who spent sixteen years in South Africa as a missionary, found some of father's relatives, and one of his brothers, supposed to be over ninety years old, gave her a great deal of information concerning our family history.

After a diligent search of over fourteen years for the different members of our family, nine children met with mother and held what today would be known as a family reunion, but then we called it a three days' feast in the wilderness. Each of us had a different name. Our missionary aunt was with us, and after her explanation to us of how father was brought away in slavery we decided to establish a family name and record. After carefully talking it over, a unanimous vote was taken to discard all other names and hereafter answer to our father's name, which meant Robinson. I am prouder of my father's heathen name than of all the professed christian names that I was compelled to acknowledge while a slave. I pray God that none of us who bear the name of our father will ever bring dishonor to it, and may God help my daughter and me to carry the gospel to his native land.

Will you help us by purchasing our book?

Yours for Christ and Africa.
W. H. ROBINSON.

A RETROSPECTION.

It is now 48 years since the greatest of all the wars has closed. Today the muskets of the soldiers - North and South - are stacked, and we entwine our wreath of flowers about them, and look upon them with much reverence - truly relics of other days - days that must live in our memory only, for this is another age. But as we look on them we are reminded that this great country could never have attained its present status without this great conflict. So we have a wreath placed on these old guns and tender memories for the boys both North and South who carried them. Our country needed the sacrifice - you gave your lives and we are sure that the "God of Battles" will give you the reward.

THE OLD ORGAN USED IN THE SONG SERVICE
OF REV. ROBINSON'S MEETINGS.

CHAPTER XXVII.

KEEPING THE CHARGE OF THE LORD.

A charge to keep I have,
A God to glorify;
A never crying soul to save,
And fit it for the sky;

To serve the present age,
My calling to fulfill;
O may it all my powers engage,
To do my Master's will!

Arm me with jealous care,
As in Thy sight to live;
And O, Thy servant, Lord, prepare,
A strict account to give!

Help me to watch and pray,
And on Thyself rely,
Assur'd if I my trust betray,
I shall for ever die.

SERMON ON "THE EXALTATION OF CHRIST."

Text. Philippians, 2nd, 9, 10, 11.

"Wherefore God also hath highly exalted Him, and given Him a name which is above every name, that at the name of Jesus every knee should bow, of things in heaven and things in earth, and things under the earth and that every tongue should confess that Jesus Christ is Lord to the Glory of God the Father."

The text represents Christ as the most exalted Being in existence. The cause which moved the pen of inspiration to this divine utterance grew out of a consideration of the degraded and relapsed condition of the church at Philippi, a famous city of the province of Macedonia, situated on the great highway between Thrace and Anapolis.

It was founded possibly by the descendants of Jashet, through the line of Gomer. Philip, the king of the province, remodeled it and gave it its present name, after which it became the metropolis of Western Asia. It was also noted for the products of gold, silver, etc., in whose mines men were engaged in great numbers, thousands of feet beneath the surface. This lucrative traffic brought to Philippi strangers from every nation, hence the city became the central point of scholastic lore and the strong hold of Grecian mythology. Paul had visited this empire of Paganism, A. D. 52, organized the church, and preached Christ unto them, etc.

Date and occasion of the Epistle to the Philippians, A. D., 62. Paul found himself a prisoner at Rome, where he had been sent from Caesasea for trial in the Roman court. The church at Philippi on learning of his imprisonment raised a collection for him and sent it by Epaphroditus, their minister, who on his arrival at Rome called at the jail, where he found the object of his mission with a chain around his waist and ankle, and hard at work on a tent, for he was a tent maker by trade. The preacher from Philippi informed Paul of the relapsed and degenerated condition of his church in the polluted city of Philippians. Object of the epistle was, first to encourage and confirm the faith of the church in Christ Jesus. Second, to caution it against idolatry and heathen mythology. Third, he warns them to shun Judaizing teachers, and fourth, he sets forth the Divinity of Christ and the exalted position of His dual nature, the last of which is the theme of our discourse, "The Exaltation of the Humanity of Christ."

May we not pause a moment, and with unshod feet approach the holy ground of this sacred mystery, and inquire into this sublime and peerless act of exaltation of humanity? On the last day of creation man was left at the foot of the ladder of the intelligent being, just a little lower than the angels, but the language of the text through the hyposative union clothes him with divinity, lifts him far above all creatures, and makes him a life member of the triune God

Head, hence the union of the divine, and human nature stands without a parallel in the annals of events. For this mysterious act the invisible curtains of divinity were drawn back, and the human soul thrown upon the dissecting table of infinite wisdom. The infinity of days steps behind the screen of his incomprehensibleness, stoops and absolves himself into the spiritual and carnal elements of the finite, passes under the fierce rod of chastisement, enters Joseph's tomb, binds the king of terrors to his chariot wheel and leads to captivity the captive, and gives gifts unto men by removing Eden to Paradise, and the renewal of the moral image of God in the soul by the indwelling of the Holy Spirit.

> Hosanna to our conquering King.
> All hail Incarnate Love,
> Ten thousand songs and glories wait
> To crown Thy head above.

> Thy victories and thy deathless flame
> Through all the world shall run,
> And everlasting ages sing
> The triumphs Thou hast won.

For through the incarnation man and God are brought face to face; by the death and resurrection they are made friends, and man is placed in a position where he can leap from the eventful stage of immortality to the drama of the immortal, where he can stand in the blazing light of the throne and see Jesus, the second Adam, clothed in divine majesty and ruling the world. Wherefore God also hath highly exalted him, and given him a name which is above every name, that at the name of Jesus every knee should bow, of things in heaven, and things in earth and things under the earth, and that every tongue should confess that Jesus Christ is Lord to the glory of God the Father. Things in heaven. Where is heaven, and what are the things referred to in the text? The poet answers the first in the following lines:

> "There is a land far away amid the stars
> Where they know not the sorrow of time,

Where the pure waters wander through valleys of gold,
And life is a treasure sublime.

Our gaze cannot soar to that beautiful land
But our visions have told of its bliss,
And our souls by the gates of its garden are fanned,
When we faint in the desert of this."

The didactive import of the above delineation directs the eyes of the soul at once to the center of the universe, the sensorium of the Godhead, the home of the angels; a city with blazing walls, and towering spires, shining domes and pearly gates, and whose streets are paved with gold, upon which the feet of the redeemed walk, and where cherubic legions dance upon a sea of glass all mingled with fire, and phalanx of seraphim bask in the golden sunlight of the city of God. These are the things which are in heaven, and they have been described and classified by Dr. Bright, as follows: First, the seraphim, whose duty it is to give glory to God as creator of all things, acknowledging his triune character by crying, Holy, Holy, Holy, Lord God of hosts, the whole earth is full of Thy glory. Second, the cherubim. They form the highest order of intelligent creatures, stand in an especial nearness to God, and are engaged in the loftiest adoration and are associated with the mercy seat. Third: This is a superior order of angels, who, under the command of Gabriel, stand as connecting links between God, as creator, and Jesus Christ as mediator, between God and man. Fourth: The fourth is under Michael, the angel liaison of heavens. Warriors who fought the dragon and threw him over the battlement of heaven, down nine times the space that measures day and night to mortal men. The fifth order is under the supervision of Uriel. They compose the fire department, and execute vengeance upon the earth by hurling forth sheeted flames of red tongued lightning and hot thunder bolts, and belching out liquid and sulphurious flames from burning craters. The sixth order is commanded by the angel Raphael. They are the health officers of the world. The seventh and last is composed of the glorified saints of all ages. The general assembly and church of the first born, which are written in heaven, and the spirits of just men made perfect. All the above are the things which are in heaven, and they are the ones who are commanded in the text to bow at the name of Jesus, for we read in the gospel of peace, that when the incarnate feet of the immaculate touched the Bethlehemic manger chanting legates from glory came to proclaim the Savior's name, the sound was heard upon the plane that God and man were reconciled again. [Things in earth.] "In surveying the great system of nature with a christian and philosophic eye, it may be considered from a different point of view," says the learned Dr. Dick. Hence, in explaining this part of the text, we shall start from a scientific point by noticing, first, the surface of the earth, second, the atmosphere. The student of science is confronted upon the threshold of his observation with countless phenomena, all dissimilar one from another, yet controlled by law of the survival of the fittest. The surface of the earth contains a multiplicity of objects all dissimlar in shape, size, color, motion and substance; craggy cliffs and towering mountains, verdant hills arrayed with clumps of trees and beds of flowers, broad and spacious plains, dotted with cities, towns and hamlets, waving fields of grain, blooming vineyard, meandering rivulets, flowing streams, roaring cataracts and belching volcanoes, bubbling springs, stagnated ponds, spacious lakes and rolling rivers. But let me lengthen the horoscope of imagination a little. Go see the outlines of a picture whose phenomenal background is far more sublime than the one whose negative lingers in the mental camera of the vision. See the erect form of him who is made in the image of his creator, and around him are gathered the rational and intelligent children of his flesh and blood, beneath whose shadow fifty thousand animal species are leaping and dancing. They are all sizes, from the mite to the elephant, from the creatures of which, if ten thousand of them were united they would not form an object one half the size of a grain of sand; yet all of these animals have organs, joints, limbs, feet, claws, hoofs, wings, fins; some flying, some crawling, some rolling, some walking on two feet, some on four, some on eight and some on eight thousand. Some with two eyes, some with ten thousand. These are some of the things in the earth. Now the chief. Hence, after he fell the whole creation groaned and travailed in pain together, until Calvary's bleeding conqueror burst the seals of Joseph's new tomb and sent up a shout of victory from the church militant to the church triumphant.

"Look, ye saints, the sight is glorious,
See the man of sorrow now,
From the fight returns victorious,
Every knee to Him shall bow.
Hark! those loud triumphant chords!
Jesus takes the highest station,
O what joy the sight affords."

The atmosphere is teeming with rational spirits, sent from God to look after the souls of men. The air we breathe swarms with legions of invisible insects, every drop of water abounds with millions of living beings. The blood is a living stream of insects, crawling and flowing through the trunk of the animal kingdom, and for aught we know these insects are the underlying principles of our intelligence, for they work on and on from birth until death, as though they were conscious of what they were doing. Hence, these and the spirits in the air, are called upon to bow at the name of Jesus.

CHAPTER XXVIII.

SUBJECT, PRAYER - LUKE 18: - 1.

Sermon delivered in Allen Chapel, Kansas City, Missouri, July 15th, 1906, by Rev. W. H. Robinson.

"And he spake a parable unto them to this end, that men ought always to pray, and not to faint. Who can pray so that God will hear?" First Ps., 66: - 18. "If I regard iniquity in my heart the Lord will not hear me." It means to look at "with favor," to "respect," "approve," "regard." God will not hear the man who in his heart looks upon sin with any favor or allowance. God looks at sin with abhorence. He is of purer eyes than to behold evil, and cannot look on iniquity, etc. We must have the same attitude toward sin that He has to be heard of Him. If we regard sin He will not regard us when we pray. Herein lies the very simple explanation why many of us pray and are not heard. Second Prov. 28-29. "He that turneth away his ear from hearing the law, even his prayer shall be abomination." He cannot pray so that God will hear. If we turn our ears away from what God says to us in His law, He will turn His ears away from what we say to Him in our prayers. We have an illustration of this in Zach. 7-11-13. "But they refused to hearken and pulled away the shoulder, and stopped their ears that they should not hear. Yea, they made their hearts as an adamant stone lest they should hear the law and the words which the Lord of Hosts hath sent."

In His spirit by the former prophets, therefore came a great wrath from the Lord of Hosts. Then it came to pass as He cried and they would not hear, so they cried and I would not hear, saith the Lord of Hosts. Many are saying: "The promises of God are not true, God does not hear my prayer." Has God ever promised to hear your prayer? God plainly described the class whose prayers He hears. Do you belong to that class? Are you listening to His words? If not He has distinctly said He will not listen to your prayers. And in not listening to you He is simply keeping His word. Let us notice (Prov. 1: 24-25-28, R. V.) "Because I have called and you have refused! I have stretched out my hand and no man regarded. But ye have set at naught all my counsel and would none of my reproof Then shall they call upon me, but I will not answer; they shall seek me diligently but they shall not find me." Third, Prov. 21-13. "Whoso stoppeth his ears at the cry of the poor, he also shall cry but shall not be heard." Third proposition: "Whosoever stoppeth his ears at the cry of the poor cannot pray so God will hear. If we will not listen to the poor when they cry unto us in their need, the Lord will not hearken unto us. The world's maxim is, "the Lord helps those who help themselves." Luke 18-9-10-11-12. And he spake this parable unto certain ones which trusted in themselves that they were righteous and despised others. Two men went up into the temple to pray; the one a Pharisee. and the other a Publican. The Pharisee stood and prayed thus with himself; "God I thank thee that I am not as other men are; extortioners, unjust, adulterers, or even as this Publican. I fast twice in the week, I give of all that I possess."

The truth is, the Lord helps those who help others. Fourth, Luke 18-13-14. "And the Publican standing afar off would not lift up so much as his eyes unto heaven, but smote upon his breast, saying, God be merciful to me a sinner." I tell you this man went down to his house justified rather than the other, for "every one that exalteth himself shall be abased, and he that humbleth himself shall be exalted." This prayer itself is the first act of faith. The first and most natural and most proper thing for one who honestly wishes to turn from sin and believe on Christ and to be saved, is to pray. The Lord Jesus looked on with delight when he could say to Ananias of the stubborn rebel, Saul of Tarsus, "behold he prayeth." Acts 9-11. "And the Lord said unto him, arise and go into the street which is called Straight, and inquire in the house of Judas for one called Saul of Tarsus, for behold he prayeth."

We should be sure, however, that the sinner really is sorry for sin, and really wishes to forsake it before we tell him to pray for pardon. You can get him on his knees even before this, and so get him to realize that he is in God's presence, so that his rebellious heart may be humbled, but do not have him pray until he really does wish to turn from sin.

Fourth Proposition. The great sinner who is sorry for and humbled by his sin, and who desires pardon, can pray so that God will hear. The question is often asked, "shall we get unconverted people." If a man is sorry for his sin and wishes to forsake it and find mercy, and is willing to humble himself before God and ask for pardon, he is taking the very steps by which a man turns around, or is converted. To tell a man he must not pray under such circumstances, is to tell him that he must not be converted until he is converted, that he must not turn until he is turned round. To get him to pray is just the thing to do, "for whosoever shall call upon the name of the Lord shall be saved. (Rom. 10-3). But how, some one may ask, can he pray until he has faith? The answer is very simple, hence the necessity of prayer. The text says, men ought always to pray and not to faint. You see when the Lord commanded Ananias to go to the house of Judas, how he shook and trembled and even reminded the Lord of the fact that Saul had come there on a mission of persecution, and at that very moment he had letters of authority from the High Priest to bring back to Jerusalem all that he found calling on the name of Jesus, but when he was informed by the great High Priest and captain of our salvation, that "behold he prayeth," it destroyed every vestige of fear, and he went rejoicing on his mission and greeted him as brother Saul, and Saul laid his desire before Him at once, and that was that His eyes might be opened. It was a prayer from an humble and contrite heart. Hence it was answered. He told him how he was struck blind on the way from Jerusalem to Damascus. He told of the blazing magnetic sun light that shone in his pathway. He told of the voice that spake unto him, (Acts 9-4.) He told of his answer (Acts 5.) It was Saul's first real prayer, though it took the heavy rod of chastisment to bring him to it. God heard and answered his prayer, and will hear yours, sinner, if you will humble yourself before Him. As soon as Paul received strength he began to preach redemption through the blood of Christ. (notice Rom. 1-16). For I am not ashamed of the gospel of Christ; for it is the power of God unto salvation to every one that believeth; to the Jew first and also to the Gentile. Hence, men ought always to pray and not to faint. Prayer is the key that unlocks heaven's door, and gives man a foreglimpse of that house not made with hands, and brings him back into full unity with his Father who art in heaven. It takes him back through the moulds of God's eternal power, and restores the image that was defaced by sin into the likeness of his creator. "For, as in Adam, all die; even so in Christ shall all be made alive." (1st Cor. 15-22).

In the year of 1871, when the gold fever was at its height in Cheyenne, Wyoming, two young men, inspired by the thought of wealth, sacrificed everything, left home and friends for the wilds of that unsettled territory, seeking their fortune. They were quite fortunate and obtained considerable gold, but their anxiety is greater now than it was when they were going, for they were not afraid of losing their lives when they had no gold, but now they are in constant fear. Therefore they had to be on the alert day and night for fear of the band of robbers who would murder them for their gold. Hence one would walk his beat with gun in hand, with a vigilant eye, while the other slept, and vice versa, and they continued this for twenty-eight days until they finally reached the border states. One night the picket discovered a dim light in the distance, quietly awoke his partner and prepared to defend themselves from their supposed enemies. Upon reconnoitering they soon discovered they had reached the border of civilization, and that the dim light discovered was the home of an old christian man and his wife, who were only too glad to give them shelter, and food such as they had. After supper they went up in the loft to go to bed, but not being fully satisfied of their safety, neither undressed. One slept with rifle in hand, while the other sat at the head of the stairs as a sentinel until a late hour in the night, when the angelic voice of the old mother was heard singing one of Zion's praises. The sentinel sprang to his feet, with joy in his soul, as she continued to sing:

"I'm a poor wayfaring stranger,
While journeying through this world of woe,
Yet there's no sickness, toil nor danger,
In that bright world to which I go.

I'm going there to see my father,
I'm going there no more to roam.
I'm just a going over Jordan
I'm just a going over home."

He rushed to the bed, shook his partner, saying: "John, come here quick." His partner seized his gun and started, but he said, "John, lay down your gun and listen." The old folks continued to sing:

"I know dark clouds will gather round me.
I know my way is rough and steep.
Yet brighter fields lie just before me,
Where God's redeemed their vigil keep.

I'm going there to see my mother,
She said she'd meet me when I come.
I'm just a going over Jordan,
I'm just a going over home."

In a moment they stood in silence in each other's arms, with their hearts overflowing with joy. When the silence was broken one said to the other, "John, that sounds like our mothers in old Indiana." About this time the old mother sang the last verse.

"I'll soon be free from every trial,
My body will sleep in the old church yard.
I'll drop the cross of self denial,
And enter on my great reward.

I'm going there to see my Savior,
To sing His praise in heaven's dome;
I'm just a going over Jordan
I'm just a going over home."

After this the old mother prayed one of those earnest, fervent prayers, asking God to watch over and protect the strangers in their home. John said to his partner, "let's undress and go to bed for we're all right; we are in a praying home."

Men ought always to pray and not to faint. Paul, the great Gentile preacher, with Silas, his brother, was cast into the Philippian jail for preaching Christ as the only hope of salvation. They were thrust into prison with their feet in the stocks. (Acts 16-22-28th verse). Paul might have asked this question of his companion; "why do we stay in this dungeon, with our feet in the stocks and our backs bleeding? Where is the Christ that met me on the highway to Damascus? Where is the God of our fathers, Abraham, Isaac and Jacob, who trusted in God and conquered every foe? He has promised not to leave nor forsake us." Let us sing one of the songs of Zion, after which they prayed until the heavens vibrated and reverberated with the prayers of these saints, and God sent down some of heaven's embassadors, some of the swift winged messengers, and as they hovered above that prison the prison was shaken from center to circumference, and the bolts and bars were loosened, and God unlocked the shackles and manacles that held them in the stocks, and they walked out into the corridor of the jail praising God in the highest. The jailer felt the shaking of the prison as a mighty earthquake. He rushed into the prison and seeing the doors all opened, and seeing no man he drew his sword and would have taken his own life, for it was certain death for a Roman soldier to allow a prisoner to escape. But Paul cried with a loud voice, saying; "Do thyself no harm, for we are all here." Then he called for a light, and sprang in and came trembling and fell down before Paul and Silas and brought them out, and said, "Sirs, what must I do to be saved?" And they said, "believe on the Lord Jesus Christ and thou shalt be saved, and thy house," and that night the Philippian jailer and his house were converted and baptized unto God, the result of prayer.

Men ought always to pray and not to faint.

"Prayer is the soul's sincere desire,
Unuttered or expressed,
The motion of a hidden fire
That trembles in the breast -
Prayer is the simplest form of speech
That infant lips can try;
It lifts us from the mire and clay
And plants our feet on high.
Oh, Thou, by whom to God, we come,

From Log Cabin to the Pulpit; or, Fifteen Years in Slavery

The truth, the life, the way,
The path of prayer Thyself hath trod,
Lord, teach us how to pray."

CHAPTER XXIX.

SUBJECT, STANDARD.

Sermon delivered by Rev. W. H. Robinson, Albia, Iowa, A. M. E. Church, March 28th, 1907.

"Go through, go through the gates, prepare ye the way of the people, cast up, cast up the highway, gather out the stones, lift up a standard for the people." This is the prophet's fervent zeal for God's promises to his church. Ministers are incited to like importunity. Isaiah, the son of Amos, prophesied B. C. 760 years, or about that time. God has had a man for every time, emergency and purpose. When He would raise up a people to Himself, he called Abraham, a Chaldean. When He would preserve that people's life He prepared a Joseph. When He would lead those people to a land of promise he called a Moses, a fugitive from Egypt. When He heard the cries from the Babylonian captives, who cried by reason of their sore affliction, he had a Nehemiah. When he heard the cries of the slaves in the southland He called in Abraham Lincoln, from the Log Cabin in Kentucky, to be the chief magistrate of this great nation. Although the nation was baptized in human blood, and Lincoln died the death of a martyr, he became the great standard of liberty in America. When the voices of the Cubans and the Philipinoes reached the throne of our God He gave to us a William McKinley, who dared to do and to die because he was inspired by the Holy Ghost, all of whom became great standards for God and suffering humanity.

Isaiah declared for Zion's sake he would not hold peace, and for Jerusalem's sake I will not rest until the righteousness thereof go forth as brightness, and the salvation thereof as a lamp that burneth and the Gentiles shall see their righteousness and all Kings thy Glory, and thou shalt be called by a new name which the mouth of the Lord shall name. Thou shalt also be a crown of glory in the hands of the Lord and a royal diadem in the hand of thy God. This subject has a two-fold meaning; a spiritual and literal. The spiritual and literal. The spiritual, Isaiah points the people to the coming King, and said to his kingdom there should he no end. [See Isaiah 9-6.] For unto us a child is horn, unto us a son is given, and the government shall he upon His shoulders, and His name shall be called wonderful counselor, the almighty God, the everlasting father, the Prince of Peace. (Isaiah 9-7: Of the increase of His government and peace there shall be no end. Upon the throne of David and upon his kingdom, to order it anti to establish it with judgment and with justice from henceforth, even forever. (See Isaiah 63; 1st to 6th verses). Who is this that cometh from Edom with dyed garments from Bozrah? This that is glorious in his apparel, traveling in the greatness of his strength? I that speak in righteousness mighty to save. Wherefore art thou red in thine apparel, and thy garments like him that treadeth in the wine fat? I have trodden the wine-press alone and of the people.

There was none with me, for I will tread them in my fury, and their blood shall be sprinkled upon my garments, and I will stain all my raiments, for the day of vengeance is in my heart, and the year of my redeemed is come. And I looked and there was none to help, and I wondered that there was none to uphold; therefore mine own arms brought salvation unto me, and my fury it upheld me, and this is the great standard that was to be a light to the feet of the Gentiles, and a lamp to the pathway that was to shine away the darkness of the valley of the shadow of death. (Text) "Go through, go through the gates, prepare ye the way of the people. Cast up, cast up the highway, gather out the stones, lift up a standard for the people." The four gates to the garden of Eden were closed by the fall of Adam. The four gates of the city of New Jerusalem were opened by the birth, suffering death, resurrection, and ascension of the Lord Jesus Christ. For death reigned from Adam to Christ, but life shall reign from time to eternity, for Jesus said (St. John 11:25). "I am the resurrection and the life, he that believeth in me, though he were dead, yet shall he live (26th) and whosoever liveth and believeth in me shall never die." (See Matthew 3: 1st to 4th verses.) "In those days came John the Baptist preaching in the wilderness of Judea, and saying, repent ye, for the kingdom of Heaven is at hand. For this is he that was spoken of by the prophet Isaiah, saying, the voice of one crying in the wilderness, prepare ye the way of the Lord. Make His path straight." John was the great standard of righteousness in the wilderness. Then cometh Jesus from Gallilee to Jordan unto John to be baptized of him. But John forbade Him, saying, "I have need to be baptizied of thee; and cometh Thou to me?" And Jesus answering said unto him: "Suffer it to be so now, for thus it becometh us to fulfill all righteousness." Then He suffered Him, and Jesus, when he was baptized, went up straightway out of the water, and lo the heavens were opened unto Him, and He saw the spirit of God ascending and descending like a dove and lighting upon Him, and lo, a voice from heaven saying, this is thy beloved Son, in whom I am well pleased.

And this is the standard that Isaiah saw through the spirit more than 760 years before he came, and prophesied concerning Him. Priests and prophets prayed to see the light of the coming king, who was to redeem Israel from the curse of a broken law, for the sentence of death was passed upon all men. Therefore (Job 14- 14) ask this question: "If a man die shall he live again?" And Jesus, the standard of salvation, answered and said, "because I live ye shall live also." (John 14-19.) And he said unto Mary and Martha, the two orphan girls who had lain their only brother in the silent city of the dead and were now kneeling at the feet of Jesus and bewailing their loss, when Martha said unto Him, "if thou hadst been here my brother had not died, but I know that even now whatsoever thou ask of God, God will give it thee," Jesus said unto her, "thy brother shall rise again." "Martha said unto Him, "I know that he will rise again in the resurrection at the last day." Jesus said unto her, "I am the resurrection and the life, he that believeth in me, though he were dead yet shall he live:" (John 11 -21 and 25th verses). So the world need not worry or have any fear concerning eternal life, for God has so declared that before one jot or tittle of His word shall fail, heaven and earth shall pass away. (Rev. 21:1-3). And John declared "he saw a new heaven and a new earth, for the first heaven and the first earth were passed away, and there was no more sea, and I, John, saw the holy city, New Jerusalem, coming down from God out of heaven, prepared as a bride adorned for her husband." And we know that it must have been a beautiful sight that dazzled the eyes of the most expectant. "And I heard A great voice out of heaven saying, behold, the tabernacle of God is with men, and He will dwell with them and they shall be His people, and God himself shall be with them and be their God." This is a glorious promise. This destroys the very fear of death from the minds of God's true pilgrims, so that they wade out into the turbulent waters of the valley and shadow of death, and, like David the shepherd king, defy the presence of death. And as he sees the approaching of the grim monster, he buckles on armour, his habiliment, girds up his loins - with a girdle of God's eternal truth, tries his shield that bears the marks of many spears shot at him by the enemy, unsheathes his sword and marches out to meet the last enemy to be conquered, which is death.

Hush! I hear the din of the battle. It is fierce, long and loud. The combatants on one side are fighting for truth and righteousness; the other side for death and destruction. The captain on one side is Apolian, the prince of the powers of the air. The other one is the Alpha and Omega. the beginning and the end, the first and the last, who conquered the powers of death and hell, robbed the grave of her victory and death of its sting, mounted the clouds of the morning with a convoy of angels as his escort, soared back to his father's house with a promise of another comforter to the world, and sitteth at the right hand of God the Father Almighty, where he maketh intercession for the Saints.

The great standard of righteousness, the literal side of the prophet's definition, points to the Babylonian captivity. Looking down through the telescope of time, he sees the Israelites, the chosen people of God, the Abrahamic seed, 767 years before the event really takes place, led away from Jerusalem, and their native land, by Nebuchadnezzar, king of Babylon, captives. Isaiah heard the echo of their wails, and the deep groaning of their souls as they are marching from their native land destined to a life of servitude which must last for 70 years. They yet bear the scars and sore feet of weary years of an Egyptian bondage, where they toiled 450 years under Pharaoh, the King of Egypt. Led out by Moses, God's standard bearer, they could hear the hoof and steel of Pharaoh's horses and chariots. They could hear the stern command of that mighty king, urging his army on to overtake them. I can hear their wails to Moses, their leader and standard bearer. I can see Moses, God's standard bearer, as he goes to headquarters for orders, as he listens to the tramp of his enemies, and the rumbling of their chariot wheels. He makes this inquiry; "Lord, what shall I do?" God said to him; "tell the people to stand still and see the salvation of God, for the enemy you see today you shall soon see them no more forever." He commanded Moses to take the staff that he had in his hand, and pass it three times over the waters of the Red Sea, and the water became frightened at itself, for God sent down a trade wind that night and divided the water from the water. Having thus pontooned the Red Sea, dry land appeared, and the people marched over dry shod. God put a pillar of cloud by day and a pillar of fire by night, so it was darkness to the Egyptians by day and by night, but light to the Israelites. When Israel had crossed the Red Sea and the Egyptians attempted to do the same, God spoke to the waters, and the Egyptians were destroyed. Israel looked back, and sang this triumphant song:

"Isaac, a ransom while he lay
Upon the altar bound;
Moses, an infant cast away,
By Pharaoh's daughter found.

Didn't old Pharaoh get lost,
Get lost: get lost?
Oh, didn't old Pharaoh get lost,
All in the Red Sea?"

Said they, the horseman and his rider are over-thrown, and God has delivered his people from the hand of Pharaoh?"

[Text] Lift up a standard for the people. They wandered forty years in the wilderness. They were unfaithful and unthankful. They murmured and complained all the time. When they were hungry, God fed them bread made up by the spoken word of His Power and fed it to them fresh and flakey every morning. And Jesus says I am the bread of life. Jesus is to the soul what the manna was to the body of the Israelites. For forty years they wandered in the wilderness, because of their disobedience, and today the church of God is wandering because of retrogration from the true standard of God. We are taking on too much of the world, and too little of God. Israel's sins led them into many pitfalls. Finally they were bitten by the fiery serpents, and died by the thousands. God commanded Moses, the standard bearer, to mould a serpent of brass and lift it up in the wilderness and to tell the people to look upon it and they should be healed. But thousands died because they would not look. Jesus said, "as Moses lifted up the serpent in the wilderness, even so must the son of man be lifted up." As the great standard of the human family, the Lord help us to look and live. Sinners, which will you do? Look and live, or close your eyes and die? (Text) Lift up a standard for the people. (See illustration). In 1869 your humble servant made a trip to London, England. While there I met a German whose sympathy was very strong for me and my people in this country, and we were together nearly every day while there. He had been a sailor for forty years, and I being a natural born mariner it blended us very close together. We would stand upon the pier of that great harbor, where we could see the white winged doves of commerce coming from every civilized quarter of the earth, and as I saw the different flags at the mastheads I would say to my friend. "where does that ship come from?" Without waiting to read the inscription on the ensign he would say, "from Italy". "And this one?" "from France." "And this?" from Germany." "And this?" from Russia." "And this" "from Spain etc." But when I saw the old star spangled banner I did not have to ask any questions. I knew it was the standard that was unfurled over me at Blue Springs, Tennessee. In November, 1863, just after being captured from the confederate army, General Thomas had me stand in the door of his tent, and ordered the national flag unfurled. It was very calm, not a breath of air stirring, but just as General Thomas stepped to my side it seemed as if God sent a providential breeze along, and it wrapped the old flag all around us. General Thomas, who controlled the union army of the Tennessee said, "today this flea makes you a free man." I wept for joy, standing under the great standard of liberty, for I could now sing the national air, the land of the free and the home of the brave. In the true sense of patriotism I had worn the shackles of literal bondage for years, but in due season God emancipated me from being the goods and chattels of other men, so I could think and act for myself as a man. But thanks be to God, in 1877, he emancipated my soul from the bondage of sin.

When I saw the standard of America I asked no questions. So it ought to he with every true child of God, who has been freed from the bondage of sin, and made heirs and joint heirs of the Lord Jesus Christ and become such lofty standards that we would be living epistles, read and known of all men as the standards of Jesus. (Text). Lift up a standard for the people. There are so many ways we can be standards. First, by faithfulness to the cause we represent. Second, by our Christian fidelity, truth and righteousness. Love God supremely. Be at peace with all men. In order to do this we must keep aloft the standard of prayer, which is a weapon sharper than any two edged sword. It is a standard of power that even the heathen in the jungles of Africa recognize and reverence, though their deity is nothing but a dumb idol. They bow down to it and utter some form of prayer. Hence we can see the necessity of the standard of prayer. (See illustration). In 1871 this country sent a representative to Madrid, Spain. In the Spanish courts they found some technicality in the official acts of Mr. Woods. They gave him a trial and sentenced him to death, and within three days of the time of execution the law said, a man sentenced to death must be executed the very day and minute specified in his sentence. If not, it gave him sufficient grounds for a new trial. The honorable James G. Blaine was at that time secretary of war, and saw the necessity of prolonging the time, so that Mr. Woods could have a fair and impartial trial, that he might vindicate himself. He asked Queen Victoria, of England, to order her representatives, with the flag of her country, to be on the spot of execution. He also made the same request to the czar of Russia. He ordered an American representative, with the stars and stripes, with the other nations, and a few minutes before the time of execution they wrapped Mr. Woods up in these three flags. Twenty four men, with loaded guns, are waiting for orders to send the leaden messenger of death into the body of Mr. Woods. The time is up. Attention is called But there is no command to fire. The question is asked, "why don't you give the command to shoot? The time is up." The answer is, "how can we shoot a man through the flags of three great nations?" The time of execution is past. Mr. Woods was taken back to prison, had a fair and impartial trial, and was set at liberty. Now, if the standards of three nations can save a man from a literal death, what must the standard of Calvary do? Every strand of thread in that flag is stained in the blood of Calvary's lamb. And Jesus said unto the dying thief, "today shalt thou be with me in paradise." (Text): Lift up the standard for the people. He was crucified, dead and buried. The third day he arose from the dead, and said, "I am he that liveth, and was dead, and behold I am alive forevermore, and have the keys of death and hell. Amen."

MY THANKS BE UNTO YOU.

The following are a few voluntarily contributed testimonials by friends who have read my life's history work entitled, "From Log Cabin to the Pulpit," all of which I most heartily appreciate and extend my sincere and earnest thanks to those who have thus taken such warm interest in both myself and daughter, and in the work we are endeavoring to accomplish for humanity through the aid of and in the name of the Lord Jesus Christ, our Savior, and the Savior of all mankind who wish his help and are willing to follow him and his teachings. God extends his help to all.

W. H. ROBINSON.

EAU CLAIRE, WIS., JULY 8, 1913.

TO WHOM IT MAY CONCERN:

I have been personally acquainted with Rev. W. H. Robinson, of this city, for several years. I have read his book, "From Log Cabin to the Pulpit," which contains his life's history and reminiscences of the Civil war, which gave him his freedom from slavery, and I cannot recommend either him or his publication too highly, and hope all my friends will read this history of his life.

Respectfully Yours,
G. E. CLARK, D. D. S.

EAU CLAIRE, WIS., JUNE 14, 1913.

I believe that the story of the life of W. H. Robinson, as told by himself, is one of those interesting bits of personal history, reaching back into the slavery days of our nation. I also believe that the purpose of the man himself is high and earnest. He is trying to make his life count for the best things.

Sincerely,
A. E. LEONARD,
First Congregational Church,

EAU CLAIRE, WIS., JUNE 27, 1913.

I have known W. H. Robinson for some time, and am glad to give personal testimony to my belief in him as an earnest, honest, consecrated christian gentleman. I have not read his autobiography, but having heard him in the lecture on his life, am sure that the book will be found intensely interesting, and profitable reading.

L. E. OSGOOD,
Pastor Second Congregational Church.

EAU CLAIRE, WIS., JUNE 2, 1913.

I have read the book entitled "From Log Cabin to the Pulpit," by the Rev. W. H. Robinson, and find many interesting narrations of striking events. The book is well worthy the attention of all interested in the history of our country.

M. BENSON,
Minister in Methodist Episcopal Church.

From Log Cabin to the Pulpit; or, Fifteen Years in Slavery

CHICAGO, ILL., JUNE 27, 1910.

TO WHOM IT MAY CONCERN:

This is to certify that I am personally acquainted with Evangelist Wm. H. Robinson, who has been in this city for the past few months doing excellent service. His work in the churches of this city has been great. I therefore recommend him to the ministers of the A. M. E. Zion church or in any other field. He will render you valiant service. I am sure that whatever you may do for him will he appreciated.

His daughter is one of the sweetest singers in Israel, and a faithful christian worker. I am,

Very truly yours,
J. B. COLBERT,
Pastor of Walter's A.M.E. Zion Church
B. G. SHAW,
Presiding Elder, Chicago District,
of the Michigan Conference.

EAU CLAIRE DISTRICT   WEST WISCONSIN CONFERENCE.
LAKE STREET METHODIST EPISCOPAL CHURCH

FRANK LEE ROBERTS, PASTOR,
Residence 329 Lake Street,

EAU CLAIRE, WISCONSIN.

TO WHOM IT MAY CONCERN:

This is to certify that the Rev. Wm. H. Robinson is personally known to me as a devout, consecrated christian. and a man of considerable ability. His time is devoted to the building of God's Kingdom on earth, and his labors have been abundantly blessed. Many, because of his ministry, can testify to the saving power of Jesus Christ. I have read his book entitled, "From Log Cabin to the Pulpit" and am of the opinion that it merits a wide reading. To whomsoever this book is allowed to present its message, I predict a wider vision of true usefulness and a firmer desire to live a holy life. Such is the testimony herein that one must needs marvel at the wonderful way in which God leads the way upward for a human soul.

Sincerely yours,
FRANK LEE ROBERTS,
Pastor Lake Street Methodist Episcopal Church.

METHODIST EPISCOPAL CHURCH,
WEST WISCONSIN CONFERENCE
(EAU CLAIRE DISTRICT)
REV. S. A. BENDER, SUPERINTENDENT.

EAU CLAIRE, WIS., JUNE 6, 1913.

It is a genuine pleasure to write a word of appreciation of "From Log Cabin to the Pulpit." It is a pleasure because of the intrinsic worth of the book, and the writer's appreciation of the personal character of the author.

No one of a religious spirit can read this book without having his faith in the fact of God's providential care in the behalf of the humblest of His children greatly strengthened. The book is of worth also as a contribution to the history of the institution of slavery, and of the epoch of emancipation. This autobiography makes for optimism, and inspires the reader to a more manful fight to attain spiritual freedom. He who reads this book will be a better man for spending a time with our author in the recital of this own God guided life from slavery to freedom.

We wish for this book a large circulation, and bid it God speed on its mission.

S. A. BENDER.

From Log Cabin to the Pulpit; or, Fifteen Years in Slavery

A LETTER TO THE PEOPLE OF EAU CLAIRE, WISCONSIN.

In 1910 we became residents of Eau Claire. I want to say that I have traveled quite extensively, at home, and abroad, but I have never met such a body of warm hearted ministers as in Eau Claire; men who at once became interested in my daughter and self, and seemed to have no thought of the "black rubbing off." They belong to that class of men who look beyond the color of the skin or the texture of the hair, and they immediately extended a brotherly hand. "As the priest, so the people." Like a strong cable they have held me up. With one hand in God's, and the other in the hands of the good people in Eau Claire I could not fall.

My first service here was in the Lake Street Methodist Episcopal Church, by invitation of Rev. Guy W. Campbell and his good people. I preached four nights and gave a lecture entitled, "From Log Cabin to the Pulpit." God raised up in a very short time many, many warm hearted friends in that church. See letter of recommendation written. to Rev. C. H. Harris, pastor of the Holcombe Methodist Episcopal Church, Holcombe, Wisconsin.

LAKE STREET METHODIST EPISCOPAL CHURCH,
WEST WISCONSIN CONFERENCE,
EAU CLAIRE DISTRICT,
GUY W. CAMPBELL, PASTOR.

EAU CLAIRE, WIS., OCT. 18, 1910.

REV. C. H. HARRIS,
Holcombe, Wis.

Dear Brother: - I tried to get you by phone Sunday evening but could not. Now I will try you by letter.

I have recently had a negro and his daughter hold a few nights' services in my church. He is an ex-slave and a very good speaker. He spoke three nights in succession in my church and then gave a lecture on the subject, "From Log Cabin to the Pulpit" His sermons and lecture were good.

Now he wants to put in a few weeks around here before he goes to Texas to take up Evangelistic work there. I could get him for you for the first of next week, beginning the 24th if you desire him. He will come on this arrangement. Your church will provide entertainment, he will preach three nights and then give the lecture for 25 and 10 cents a ticket, the proceeds of which he takes as his compensation.

He was at the Salvation Army Barracks here last week, and they were so pleased with his work that they insisted on his staying this week also.

I spoke to Brother Straw last week about getting this man a few nights' appointments about here, and he immediately suggested Holcombe. He has heard him preach and give his lecture, and desired me to convey his unqualified recommendation to you.

We will not have many opportunities from now on to secure such men. Their ranks are being thinned about as fast as those of the old soldiers. This will give your young people an opportunity to hear and see a real ex-slave.

Now if you want this man write me as soon as possible. His name is W. H. Robinson. He and his daughter are fairly good singers also.

Sincerely,
GUY W. CAMPBELL.

We spent two weeks in Holcombe with the result that twenty-five were happily converted and united with the church. From there we went to other points in Wisconsin. In Eau Claire and vicinity, to date, we have seen over eight hundred people born into the Kingdom of God, for which we give Him the glory, for God forbid that I glory in anything save the cross of Christ. May God bless the people of Eau Claire for their kindness to us.

I want to thank my landlord, Mr. Stephen D. Hoover, and Mr. A. V. Mayhew, who made it possible for me to finance this edition of my history. I appreciate their true friendship. May they live long to do much good for the Master's Kingdom; also Mr. B. R. Barland, real estate man, for his untiring interest in us.

Believing that the large and fruitful work extending over a series of years by the Rev. W. H. Robinson, as an Evangelist, and his daughter assisting him as a singer, is worthy of recognition, and to the end that loyal effort, in the cause of truth and righteousness may not go unrewarded.

I believe the good people of Eau Claire will join with me in the sentiment and aid which have enabled the worthy Evangelist to publish in book form a narrative of his very interesting life; a life beginning as a slave, with its atrocious incidents; his experiences as a union soldier; the acquiring of an education, and the consecrated use of that education for the uplifting of humanity; the object of such publication being the very commendable desire to carry the gospel to his people in Africa, his father's native land.

If we as citizens, and friends of humanity, will each purchase a copy, we will certainly get value received from the contents of this valuable book, and at the same time help him to answer the call of His Master, "Go ye into all the world and preach the gospel to every creature.

B. R. BARLAND.

I wish also to thank the publisher and his helpers for the interest taken in me, and for the good work they have done in getting out a more presentable book than the former ones were. Their suggestions and help in various ways have enabled me to re-edit my book, and to bring this edition up to a higher standard.

I send this little book on its mission of love to all.

Yours for Christ,
W. H. ROBINSON.

Lightning Source UK Ltd.
Milton Keynes UK
19 January 2011

166019UK00001B/139/P